THE DISCIPLE WHOM JESUS LOVED

THE DISCIPLE WHOM JESUS LOVED

Unveiling the Author of John's Gospel

Edward Reaugh Smith

Ⓔ Anthroposophic Press

Published by Anthroposophic Press
P.O. Box 799, Great Barrington, MA 01230
www.anthropress.org

Library of Congress Cataloging-in-Publication Data

Smith, Edward Reaugh, 1932-
The disciple whom Jesus loved/Edward Reaugh Smith.
    p. cm.
Includes bibliographical references.
ISBN 0-88010-486-4 (pbk.)
    1. John, the Apostle, Saint. 2. Bible. N.T. Gospels—Criticism,
interpretation, etc. 3. Anthroposophy.

BS2455 .S54 2000
299'.935—dc21
                                                    00-026607

10 9 8 7 6 5 4 3 2 1

Printed in the United States of America

CONTENTS

INTRODUCTION

by Christopher Bamford

It is a privilege to write a few words to introduce this pithy, far-reaching essay by Edward Reaugh Smith. *The Disciple Whom Jesus Loved* focuses (with many fascinating asides) on the identity of the "beloved disciple": the one "leaning on Jesus' bosom, whom Jesus loved"—the one to whom Jesus "gave" His mother—not to mention the one who wrote the fourth Gospel, the Apocalypse, and certain letters that expound the Christian teaching of love more perfectly than any other human text. Ordinary Christians have always called this author "John," which tradition has sometimes interpreted to mean "to whom is given"[1] and which Smith tells us comes from a conflation of two Hebrew words "Yah" (or Yahweh) with "Anna," meaning "grace." In other words, John manifests and bears witness to God's grace. Certainly no Christian texts have exerted a comparable initiatory influence. Indeed, whether or not it is justifiable to speak of a "Johannine" spiritual (esoteric) Church, in contrast to the Petrine or institutional (exoteric) Church, St. John has always stood for the heights of mystical theology: the deepest Christian initiation. His identity, therefore, is a matter of more than passing interest.

This is one reason why, when asked by the New York Open Center and the Anthroposophical Society to contribute to a lecture series

---

1. John Scotus Eriugena, *Homily on the Prologue to the Gospel of St. John*, chapter 2: "O blessed John, not unworthily are you called John. The name John is Hebrew. Translated into Greek, this name means 'to whom is given.' For to whom among theologians is given what is given to you? Namely, to penetrate the hidden mysteries of the highest good and to intimate to human mind and senses what was there revealed and declared unto you. To whom else, I pray, was given grace so great and of such a kind?" (See John Scotus Eriugena, *The Voice of the Eagle: Homily on the Prologue to the Gospel of St. John* [translated with an introduction and reflections by Christopher Bamford], Hudson, New York, Lindisfarne Books, 2000.)

celebrating Christianity at the beginning of the new millennium, Ed Smith chose the theme of the identity of John: it would allow him to talk of Christian initiation in a new way, one whose time he felt had come. Another reason surely was that it allowed him to bring together a number of Rudolf Steiner's revelatory insights into New Testament study with the best of contemporary scholarship—in this case, Morton Smith's work on *The Secret Gospel of Mark*. The result is a fascinating and important little document.

Edward Reaugh Smith is not a career, academic New Testament scholar. Though he has read and studied the relevant literature, Ed has other qualifications. It is difficult to know where to begin with these, for Ed is a man of many parts and these parts cannot be easily separated. Born in Flora, Illinois—the state to which his maternal great great grandfather Richard Sprigg Canby moved from Ohio after having served with Lincoln in the Congress (another Canby was a famous Union Major General in the Civil War)—Ed is a Texan by marriage, that is to say, by "destiny" and by adoption. In 1950, freshly graduated from high school in Illinois, he met his future wife Jo Anne, a native of Wichita Falls and the daughter of a widely loved, simple but wise and deeply spiritual, chiropractor. The interplay of "nature and grace"—or "free will and destiny"—involved in finding a life's companion is always complex; and, in Ed's case, Jo Anne, the companion it gave him, sowed in his soul many seeds of insight and intuition that are still germinating and bearing fruit today. Ed and Jo Anne married in 1954 and immediately had to face Ed's induction into military service for two years. His four-year academic-test deferment had expired. This came in the middle of law school at Southern Methodist University when he stood academically at the head of his class. Typically, the two years were well used. As a result, Ed was able to complete certification as a CPA and was still able to graduate with honor from law school in 1957.

Ed's legal and accounting training served him well—and still do, as anyone will attest who has wondered at the force of argument and the mass of evidence skillfully marshalled in his magnum opus, *The Burning Bush*. More immediately, however, Ed practiced tax and estate law successfully for many years, first in Houston, and subsequently—from 1959 till 1984—in Lubbock, where he made his home and still lives today. In 1964, he acquired Resthaven Cemetery, on which he promptly built a funeral home. In this new role as businessman, Ed notes that his dominant motivation gradually but powerfully shifted from one of investment to one of community service. By the time he sold it in 1993, Resthaven had become the dominant funeral and burial facility in Lubbock, a city of 200,000 inhabitants.

During this whole period, *most importantly*, besides helping Jo Anne, "the bride of his youth," to rear two sons and a daughter, Ed taught Sunday school. Always an assiduous reader of the scriptures, Ed wrestled weekly for more than twenty-five years to satisfy heart and mind that he understood the fullness of Holy Scripture. In all, he taught the Bible through, book by book, three times.

Never narrow-minded or one-sided, Ed has honed and perfected his character in other ways, too. He ran his first marathon in January 1978 and followed this with a second in December of the same year. Finally, in April 1979, he "crowned" his running career with the Boston marathon. Having accomplished this, he reverted to the second of what Jo Anne calls his "irrational dreams": he resurrected his youthful desire to become a concert pianist. He had the irrepressible urge to know if he could perform one of the great piano concertos with an orchestra. After two years studying piano under Dr. William Westney, Browning Artist-in-Residence at Texas Tech University and winner of the Geneva International Piano Competition, Ed gave his first recital in 1981. In March of the next year, he played Beethoven's Third Piano Concerto with an orchestra before a full auditorium—thus fulfilling a lifetime ambition. He continued to give recitals for the next two years—ending with a program of Chopin and Rachmaninoff. However, as Ed himself says: "The demands of this training and performance were such that I have played no more since April 14, 1984. But the memories are rich."

All this is perhaps by the way, but it gives some measure of the man. More to our purpose was his discovery, in the fall of 1988, of the work of the philosopher, scientist, educator, and spiritual teacher, Rudolf Steiner (1861-1925). This changed his life, or at least gave his life a new direction and purpose—the writing of an "anthroposophical commentary on the Bible."

Steiner, according to the English philosopher Owen Barfield, "the best kept secret of the twentieth century," was the creator of what he called "spiritual science" or *anthroposophy*. Suffice it to say that spiritual science in Steiner's sense is a form of phenomenological research in which consciousness is both the field studied and the means of studying it *as well as* a Christian esotericism: a Christian path of inner development and an unveiling of the Christian Mystery. Steiner's vast oeuvre therefore comprehends a spiritual anthropology, cosmology, Christology, psychology, and epistemology. It includes fundamental researches into fields as varied as the Bible (especially the four Gospels, the Apocalypse, the missions of Abraham, Moses, Elijah and Paul), education, agriculture, the history of science, and medicine—to name only a few. Encountering this enormous body of work of course means different things for different people. For Edward Reaugh Smith meeting Steiner meant a "rending of the veil of the Temple." He began to understand the Bible in a new way. The meaning of many previously incomprehensible passages began to make a new sense. Even a cursory reading of the essay that follows can give one a sense of the kind of excitement that considering scripture in the light of Steiner aroused in Ed Smith. He felt he had come home.

In his talk, Ed begins by alluding to the verse in the final chapter of the Song of Solomon (8,5), which is echoed in the description of the disciple we know as John: namely, "*Who is that coming up from the wilderness, leaning upon her beloved? Under the apple tree I awakened you. There your mother was in labor with you.*" He points out that this phrase occurs after the daughters of Jerusalem have been adjured for a third time not to stir up or awaken love "*until it pleases.*" To lean upon one's beloved, therefore, is a sign that one is, in some sense, perfected in love. Then, "knowledge"—the wisdom of love that overcomes the fall or the eating of the apple, the fruit, of the tree of the knowledge of good and evil—is given. Such a person is the one known as John—but who is he?

On this vexed topic, what Ed has to say is both extraordinarily suggestive and remarkably conclusive. Covering a lot of ground, but in a way that is accessible and "reader-friendly," Ed masterfully supplies us with a range of collateral materials, always interesting in itself but also always necessary to the larger argument. I shall not steal his fire here, but only say that he deals more than adequately with the whole "Zebedee John" question and makes the case convincingly for identifying of the author of the Johannine texts with Lazarus, the rich man of Bethany (Mary Magdalene's brother), raised from the dead, for whom Jesus wept and the only specific person of whom it is written that Jesus loved.

Since this essay began its life as a talk to a non-specialized audience, it is blessedly jargon-free and reader-friendly. Yet this is not to say that it lacks sophistication or bite: it has both. Indeed, in the field of study that it addresses, it works a quiet but profound revolution. New Testament scholars as well as those concerned in a professional capacity with the future of Christianity ought therefore to sit up and take note. And not only they, of course. Anyone seeking to understand something of the mystery of Christ Jesus and his "beloved disciple" will find true food for mind and heart here.

FOREWORD

My first book, *The Burning Bush*, was published by the Anthroposophic Press in 1997. It has been described by several, both in this country and abroad, in superlatives, recognized by them as being very scholarly and of extensive scope. It is thoroughly documented throughout by extensive references, biblical and otherwise, as well as by numerous study helps. But some have suggested the need for a more simplified version of some of its topics—one that flows more easily for the average reader. *The Incredible Births of Jesus* was the first result of that endeavor. It was based upon "The Nativity" essay in *The Burning Bush*.

The Nativity was just one of the countless theological knots untied by Rudolf Steiner's intuition, his gift of prophecy. What follows in this book is another, resolving the mystery surrounding the character and identity of Evangelist John. To a large degree it is based upon the essays "Peter, James and John" and "Egypt" in *The Burning Bush*.

As mentioned in the Introduction, this book is based upon a paper I gave in New York City in November, 1999. But my choice of topic for that occasion was driven by an already existing plan for this second, simplified version from the larger book.

Consider if you will that almost the entire New Testament was written by, or under the powerful influence of, only two men, Paul and Evangelist John. Only the Gospels of Matthew and Mark and the four short letters of James, Peter and Jude fall outside their scope. Clearly the Luke-Acts combination fell under Paul's influence, and anthroposophical insights confirm ancient tradition and convincingly show Paul to have authored Hebrews and Evangelist John the book of Revelation.

The realization that the New Testament is largely a product of these two takes on added meaning when joined with the insight that these were the only two who were clearly initiated by Christ, or at least were the two most highly initiated by him—John during Christ's earthly life and Paul after his Resurrection in the episode generally known as the Damascus Road experience. The nature and consequence of initiation is touched upon in this book, though more fully described in *The Burning Bush* and the Steiner works upon which it is based. But it can be said that the high initiation each of these experienced brought insights to them from the spiritual world that have not been, and are still far from being, common within humanity. They served different missions from each other, and within their respective missions they wrote quite differently for different purposes. Paul's dominant product was the corpus of his church letters, each one focusing on an ad hoc circumstance with advice and guidance pertinent to that occasion, while his writing to the Hebrews was his more considered exposition on the meaning of the Christ mission. John also wrote letters, but they were overshadowed by the two monumental and disparate pillars of his work, the Gospel and the Apocalypse. Steiner refers to John's Gospel as the highest writing given humanity. And no book of the Bible benefits more from the prophecy of Rudolf Steiner, nor cries out for it more, than John's Apocalypse. Anthroposophy shows that it has little, if any, of the character ascribed to it by theology to date—though no book has brought greater expressions of humility or frustration from its more candid students than Revelation. To date it has belied its title. While Revelation is beyond the scope of this little book, what the reader finds here should open new windows of expectation in the student's mind as to what this spiritual giant gives us in all his writings.

Readers accustomed to more conventional theological approaches may find portions of the "Background" material unsettling at first. It will be helpful in those cases to accept these concepts tentatively until the whole story unfolds. As that happens one can thrill to the sense of the Bible taking on the image of one beautiful, integrated spiritual account consistent from beginning to end, unveiling its mysteries with wonderful new (while in fact old) meaning.

Finally, several have made the suggestion that the word "anthroposophy," not found in many English (at least American) dictionaries until quite recently, be defined. My newest dictionary, *Webster's New World College Dictionary*, 4th ed., NY, Macmillan, 1999, gives the following: "a religious or mystical system or movement similar to theosophy, founded by Rudolf Steiner about 1912." Steiner initiated his public, spiritual disclosures about 1901 under the auspices of the Theosophical Society, and as the General Secretary of its German section, and for a number of years thereafter called his work theosophy. However, his emphasis upon the centrality of the Christ Spirit in any theosophical system estranged him from the Indian Theosophists whereupon he parted from them and thereafter called his work anthroposophy. This parting occurred toward the end of the period when he focused his lectures primarily and specifically upon the Bible (generally 1908-1914). So while the above dictionary definition is generally adequate for common usage, it is not sufficiently so for more discriminating students.

Steiner coined the term "anthroposophy" for his intuitions of the spiritual world and its relation to the world we perceive with our ordinary senses. He also called it by the synonymous phrase, "spiritual science." Anthroposophy is a combination of the two Greek root words, *anthropos*, and *sophia*. The latter, with a capital, is defined in our dictionaries as "wisdom," and given a feminine attribute. The Sophia is personified as the feminine "Wisdom" in the first nine chapters of Proverbs. Our common suffix "sophy" derives from it and means "knowledge or thought," as in "philosophy," "theosophy," and the like.

Anthropos should be distinguished from *homo*, a Latin word referring to a two-legged primate. We should think of *homo* as referring to the body, and *anthropos* as referring to what sets the human being above the animal. It represents the higher aspect, the soul, or the soul and the spirit, of the human being. Thus, "anthroposophy" is the wisdom of the soul of the human being.

My larger work, of which *The Burning Bush* is Volume 1, is entitled *Rudolf Steiner, Anthroposophy and the Holy Scriptures, an*

Anthroposophical Commentary on the Bible. Its second volume, *"What Is Man?"*, should be published in 2001.

I hope and trust you will experience, as you read on, new insights enriching your own spiritual journey.

The Disciple Whom Jesus Loved

B Y THE TIME John's Gospel was written, most of the disciples who knew the author were either dead or widely dispersed. The Gospel was probably written late in the first century, but Church history shows us that by the second century, its authorship was unknown. Only because Irenaeus (A.D. 120-202), battling against the gnostics, insisted on the four Gospels based on his attribution of them to apostolic authorship, did it get into the canon, and that was based largely upon the assumption, even then shaky, that Zebedee John wrote it as one of the Twelve. In fact, especially in the light of anthroposophy, it is a virtual certainty that none of the Gospels was written by one of the original twelve disciples. Clearly Mark and Luke were not, though they gain apostolic authority from the close association of their Evangelists to Peter and Paul, respectively. Matthew and John clearly present the greatest puzzles. My little book, *The Incredible Births of Jesus*, gives Rudolf Steiner's insights into the authorship of Matthew, and in this one we will examine his views on John.

Church tradition has always accepted the fact that it was written in Ephesus by a very old man named John who lived there until his death. But for two thousand years the Church has thrown up its hands, either accepting by default that Zebedee John was its author or that its authorship is not really important. If the latter is true, then this book, which unveils that authorship, is a waste of time. I suggest to you that the time has come when it is important to know, and that the reason it is now important is that neither the Gospel nor the Bible in its entirety can be adequately understood for our time without it.

Dusting Off the Ancient Song

There is a book in the Bible we don't talk about very much any-more—it seems too blatantly sensual. For a long time its title was known as *The Song of Solomon*, but aside from both the Old and New King James and Revised Standard versions most Bibles today call it the *Song of Songs*. I will call it, and what it stands for, simply *the Song*.

Appearing immediately before *the Song* is the book of *Ecclesiastes*, only slightly more honored in our day than *the Song* but hardly any more fully understood. Probably these books are largely ignored today for the same reason that they were placed last among (or near the end of)[1] the so-called Wisdom books of the Old Testament as it took shape. The wise sage who gave us *Ecclesiastes* understood what was happening. At the outset he expresses it (Eccles 1,9-11[2]):

> [9] What has been is what will be, and what has been done is what will be done; and there is nothing new under the sun. [10] Is there a thing of which it is said, "See, this is new"? It has been already, in the ages before us. [11] There is no *remembrance* of former things, nor will there be any *remembrance* of later things yet to happen among those who come after.

The key word here is *remembrance*. It is one thing to have *remembrance* of history. It is quite another to have *knowledge* of it. The distinction between them is the key to understanding *the Song*.

There is a theme in *the Song* that occurs three times. It says, "I adjure you, O daughters of Jerusalem, that you stir not up nor awaken love until it please." But after the third of these a verse occurs that one must keep in mind when considering "the disciple whom Jesus loved, who had lain close to his breast" at the Last Supper. The verse reads, "Who is that coming up from the wilderness,[3] *leaning upon her beloved? Under the apple tree I awakened you. There*

---

1. They appear last in the Protestant Bible, but are followed by the books of *Wisdom* (or *The Book of Wisdom*) and *Ecclesiasticus* (or *The Wisdom of Ben Sira* [or *Sirach* in Greek]) in the Catholic Bible.

2. Unless otherwise noted, all biblical citations are from the Revised Standard Version.

3. According to Steiner, the term "wilderness" in the Bible is normally translated better to mean "loneliness," or "aloneness," or "solitude" or "the desolation of the soul." Careful analysis and reflection suggest he is right. See *The Burning Bush*, pp. 270-271, esp. fn 15.

your mother was in travail with you." Not only are these motifs used by John,[4] but it was only because John had attained the "love that *pleases*" in *the Song* that he could write (in regard to the promiscuous woman at Jacob's well) about the "living water" that *satisfies* in his Gospel.

There are so many things in the Bible on which theology is still totally in the dark. It has no understanding of the meaning of *Under the apple tree I awakened you.* Another is the entire book of Job, as I shall touch upon later. In its 38th chapter the Lord asks Job, "Where were you when I laid the foundation of the earth?" (vs 4) as well as a series of other questions related to ancient times and creative acts. Then it makes a very important statement, *You know, for you were born then, and the number of your days is great!* (vs 21). Later in the chapter it refers to certain stars and seems clearly to be talking about the zodiac in relation to "the ordinances of the heavens" and "their rule on the earth." The implications of all this are enormous and suggest that there is buried deep within the human soul an ancient knowledge that has been lost and needs to be remembered. This is what *the Song* is about. This is what being "awakened under the apple tree" is about.

To begin to see what it is we don't remember anymore, and so that we can grasp who this "disciple" is, it is necessary to give some background that theology has not yet given us.

Background

Rivers of ink have flowed into libraries on the topic of Evangelist John, and few aspects of these writings have been so fascinating as the question—who was he? The uniqueness and power of his Gospel are universally recognized. But his identity has remained a theological enigma to this day.

So you are right to ask how I can now presume to give an answer?

4. Three distinct motifs are involved, first "leaning upon her beloved," second "under the apple tree I awakened you," and third "There your mother was in travail with you." The meaning of each should emerge as we proceed.

There were two very important spiritual developments in the twentieth century in regard to which theology has remained for all practical purposes either oblivious or totally mute.

The first of these is the vast ocean of Steiner's intuitive revelations relative to the Bible early in the century.[5] You will come up largely empty-handed if you search theological libraries for any mention of Steiner or anthroposophy. The silence is deafening. Bibliography is endless, but this spiritual giant is never mentioned. Religions that arose out of ancient revelation now disdain any possibility of new intuitive revelation.

The second development is Morton Smith's discovery of what is known as the *Secret Gospel of Mark*.[6] Theologians are well aware of this, but not of its significance. They generally recognize Morton Smith's discovery as being an authentic letter from Clement of Alexandria[7] that makes reference to the raising of a youth from the tomb—and though he is not named, they also recognize it describes

5. Rudolf Steiner (1861-1925) is the Austrian whose works, along with my quarter century of studying and teaching the Bible in the Methodist Church, are the basis of my writings. "Anthroposophy," literally the "wisdom of the human soul," is the name (along with "spiritual science") he approved for these works. But while he was an intellectual giant by any normal means of measurement, his revelations were entirely based upon his remarkable ability to perceive in (spiritual) realms beyond the reach of normal human perception. Skeptical by nature, my own test of the reliability of his revelations was the extent to which they caused countless theological knots in biblical interpretation (hermeneutics) to dissolve into brilliant clarity of meaning.

6. Morton Smith's scholarly *Clement of Alexandria and a Secret Gospel of Mark*, Cambridge, Harvard Univ. Press, 1973, and his popular version, *The Secret Gospel*, Clearlake, CA, Dawn Horse Press, 1982 (orig. pub. NY, Harper & Row, 1973). His later updates are "Clement of Alexandria and Secret Mark: The Score at the End of the First Decade," Cambridge, Harvard Theological Review, 1982, and "Two Ascended to Heaven—Jesus and the Author of 4Q491," in *Jesus and the Dead Sea Scrolls*, NY, Doubleday, Anchor Bible Reference Library (1992).

7. (ca. A.D. 153-217), the illustrious head of the Catechetical School at Alexandria at the close of the second century, and teacher of Origen and other notables. Alexandria was the situs of the Evangelist Mark's Gospel and the earliest seat of Christian learning. It was also the home of Philo, the earlier contemporary of Christ and preeminent leader of Hellenistic Judaism who so greatly influenced the Evangelists and Paul. It is Philo's platonic concept of the Logos, "the Word," that begins John's Gospel.

Lazarus. The great significance that they fail to appreciate, however, is that together with the revelations of Steiner it shows us that Lazarus is the so-called "rich, young ruler" of all three synoptic Gospels. Steiner unequivocally identified Lazarus as the author, directly or indirectly, of the entire Johannine corpus (including the Apocalypse). And some prominent theologians, including no less than the late Raymond E. Brown, have included him among the possible authors of the Gospel and first letter. But it was not till the last half of our century that this discovery by Morton Smith at the Greek Orthodox monastery of Mar Saba in the Judean desert vindicated Steiner's assertions. At the same time it showed that Lazarus was not only the Evangelist but that he was recognized by the other three Evangelists as pre-eminent among the disciples, as reflected by their including the account of him as the "rich, young ruler." The anthroposophist Andrew Welburn, of Oxford University, in his *The Beginnings of Christianity*,[8] is, to the best of my knowledge, the first to have identified Lazarus as the "rich, young ruler," and he did so based upon the *Secret Gospel of Mark*.

I must also suggest another major significance of the *Secret Gospel of Mark* that theology has missed because it does not understand the nature of the raising of Lazarus. It is that the *Secret Gospel* resolves the great mystery of who the young man was who followed Jesus to Gethsemane wearing nothing but a linen cloth and who was seized and fled away naked. Only Mark's Gospel tells of it (Mk 14,51-52), as a consequence of which the traditional view has been that it could only describe Mark himself. But now the *Secret Gospel* suggests that he too was Lazarus/John, and not that he *actually* abandoned Jesus, but that he was able to follow him in spiritual consciousness all the way to the Cross. We shall see how this must be so as we examine the actual content of this new discovery.

Now I have jumped way ahead. And if you are a New Testament scholar or believer, not otherwise familiar with Steiner's works, you may well resist what I've suggested. So let us go back to a better starting point and work our way through.

8. Edinburgh, Floris Books, 1991, at pp. 248-250.

The source material for most of what follows is in my book, *The Burning Bush*, particularly in the two essays entitled "Peter, James and John" and "Egypt." The following chart, taken from the back of *The Burning Bush*, may be helpful to those of you not familiar with Steiner's works:

THE ESSENTIAL NATURE OF THE HUMAN BEING

As set out in Chart I-9 in *The Burning Bush*

3-Fold	4-Fold	7-Fold	9-Fold
	Physical	Physical	Physical
Body	Etheric	Etheric	Etheric
	Astral	Astral	Astral
			Sentient Soul
			Intellectual Soul
Soul		Ego	Consciousness
			(Spiritual) Soul
	Ego		
		Spirit Self	Spirit Self
		(Manas)	(Manas)
Spirit		Life Spirit	Life Spirit
		(Buddhi)	(Buddhi)
		Spirit Man	Spirit Man
		(Atma)	(Atma)

This chart encompasses the entire panorama of the evolution of the human being, and incidentally also of the lower three kingdoms. Luke's "parable" of the Prodigal Son is the story (allegory) of the descent of the human being from the spiritual world and its return thereto. This is the thesis of *The Burning Bush*, the first sentence in its General Introduction. All the lower kingdoms are by-products of the evolution of the human soul—the human being is not descended from the animal kingdom, but rather the animal and lower kingdoms are descended from the human kingdom. This is the meaning of the taking of all the animals and plants by Noah into the ark (Gen 6,19-22). This original ark is the post-Atlantean human body that has within it the residual nature of all the lower kingdoms that fell away into materiality at earlier stages of its evolution. As this pertains to the animal kingdom, Mark's Gospel portrays it with great spiritual accuracy in saying that Christ in the wilderness (meaning the solitude of the soul) wrestled with the "wild animals" (Mk 1,12), namely, the variety of untamed animal desires of the human soul.

That statement about the ark, upon reflection, already transports us to another paradigm. It condenses a chunk of *The Burning Bush* into a tiny kernel in order to get to Evangelist John.

Post-Atlantean evolution commenced with the final submergence of Atlantis about ten thousand years ago with the passage of the last ice age. The account of Noah picks up there. The speed of evolution is not consistent from one great epoch to another—I take that to be the meaning of that verse in the so-called Little Apocalypse passages of the synoptic Gospels, "And if those days had not been shortened, no human being would be saved" (Mt 24,19; Mk 13,20).[9] Evolution in the post-Atlantean epoch is divided into seven Cultural Ages related to the zodiacal signs starting with Cancer and going through Capricorn. The seven churches in John's Apocalypse (Rev 2-3) represent these seven Cultural Ages. Each Cultural Age lasts 2,160 years, one-twelfth of the time it takes

9. As reflected in the "days" of creation in Gen 1 and as implied in Prov 9,1 and in the four progressive cycles of seven in John's Apocalypse, creation (i.e., the evolution of the human being) takes place in progressions of seven, each "progression" evolving fractal-like out of its parent and telescoping into its own offspring (see *The Burning Bush*, especially charts I-1 and I-2, for a more complete portrayal). Earth evolution is thus the middle one of a seven-stage progression through what Steiner calls the Conditions of Consciousness. Earth evolution is then divided into seven "great epochs." Atlantis was the middle one of these, the fourth. Our present great epoch is the fifth, called the "post-Atlantean."

the Sun to travel the entire circuit of the heavens, 25,920 years—an astronomical fact.[10]

Moses inscribed the zodiacal twelve in the Bible when, immediately after receiving the first sacraments from Melchizedek, Abraham was first told to number the stars and that his descendants would be like them (Gen 15,5). Thus there were twelve tribes and later twelve disciples.[11] And John, also recognizing the "twelve stars" of the zodiac (Rev 12,1), brings us back to both the twelve tribes and twelve apostles when the Earth becomes spiritualized at the end of his Apocalypse.

The first two post-Atlantean Ages, Cancer and Gemini, were prehistorical (Steiner calls them "Ancient India" and "Ancient Persia,"

10. The Sun "travels" by virtue of the phenomenon called the "precession of the equinoxes." Astrological Ages, determined by such "precession," are based upon the zodiacal sign in which the Sun rises in the eastern sky at the vernal (spring) equinox. Based upon that, the Age of Aries began in 1946 B.C. and Pisces began in A.D. 215. However, there is a time lag of 1199 years between an Astrological Age and its related Cultural Age, so that the Cultural Age of Aries began in 747 B.C. and that of Pisces began in A.D. 1414. The time lag is explained in Chart I-19 in *The Burning Bush*. It also reflects the fact that transformation to a new state of human consciousness is not effected instantaneously but rather proceeds initially in a subconscious cultural impulse that manifests in a new Cultural Age only when it has reached a certain level. This spiritual phenomenon is reflected in our solar system by the fact that temperature changes on Earth lag the relationship between the Sun and the Earth. For instance, the Sun reaches it highest point in the northern hemisphere at the summer solstice in June, but the hot, dog days of summer reach their climax well over half way through the summer season. The same time lag is true with respect to cold weather in the winter.

The 25,920 years in the text is reflected in the number of times a human breathes in a day, and in the number of days in a human life (just under 71 years; cf. Ps 90,10).

11. Later the angel tells Abraham that the Lord "will multiply your descendants as the stars of heaven and as the sand which is on the seashore." But this comes only through the twelve and merely means that the twelvefoldness of the stars applies to every human soul. First there is the numbering by division into twelve, and only through that comes the multiplication. When the human being developed bones (e.g., Adam means hard) and first stood upright for the development of the skull, its cranial dome reflected the stars by dividing into twelve pairs of nerves.

respectively). The third Age was the Chaldo-Egyptian.[12] It began as memory faded and writing came into being around 3,000 B.C., the year 2,907 B.C., to be exact. This is the Cultural Age of Taurus, the Bull, that we see in Old Testament times. The patriarchs, Abraham through Joseph, fell right in the middle of this Age.

It came to an end in 747 B.C. with the pronouncement by Isaiah that for long ages we would not be able any longer to see, hear or understand in the spiritual realm (Is 6,9-13). This is the commencement of the Cultural Age of Aries, the Lamb. Christ incarnated *one third* of the way into that Age—which ended with the Renaissance, the Rebirth, of humanity in A.D. 1414. That is when the Cultural Age of Pisces, the Fishes, commenced. We are approaching *one third* of the way into that Age now. It is the Age of the Consciousness (Spiritual) Soul in the 4th column of the chart above.

There are two "feedings" in the Gospels, the five thousand and the four thousand. Matthew and Mark speak of both. John and Luke speak only of the five thousand. At that feeding, there were five loaves and two fishes. John calls this a "sign" (Jn 6,14). The two fishes are the symbol of Pisces, the five loaves for the five thousand represent the fifth Cultural Age, the Age of the Fishes. Christ, the Lamb of God, came in the Age of the Lamb. But in this passage he "lifts up his eyes" (Jn 6,5) and looks out at the future multitudes in the Age of Pisces. The significance of the sign of the fish is that it points to our Cultural Age as the time when humanity would begin to comprehend the Christ. John's Gospel was written for that Age,

---

12. It is easy to see this third Age identified as the third "church" in John's Apocalypse (Rev 2,12-17), for it speaks of the manna that relates to the time of Moses (the Chaldo-Egyptian) and also to the "I AM," the name given to the burning bush on Mt. Sinai (Ex 3,3,14). See the essay "I AM" in *The Burning Bush*. It is there shown that the proper translation of the name in Ex 3,14 is "I Am the I Am." The "new name ... which no one knows except him who receives it" (Rev 2,17) is "I Am," for no one can speak that name except the individual human soul with reference to itself. No one except myself can refer to me as "I Am," or to you as "I Am" except yourself. It is totally unique as to each individual soul. And it is especially Lazarus/John in his Gospel that relates each individual soul to the "I Am" of Christ. This is a great mystery to theology, but it is clarified in the series of essays in *The Burning Bush*.

as was his Apocalypse. We need to keep this in mind when we interpret the concluding passage about the disciple who would remain till the future time when Christ would come.

This brings us to the starting line for our mission of unveiling Evangelist John.

The first thing we must note is that he intentionally concealed his identity. Scholars widely agree that he is the one called "the disciple whom Jesus loved." The name "John" was not added to the Gospel until later in the second century—presumably by one of those few who knew its author was called John.

The reason for this concealment can best be understood when we remember that it was John's Gospel in which Jesus said, "I have yet many things to say to you, but you cannot bear them now. When the Spirit of truth comes, he will guide you into all the truth" (Jn 16,12-13).

Scholars have struggled with this passage. For just before this, Jesus had said in John's Gospel, "All that I have heard from my Father I have made known to you" (Jn 15,15).

First Jesus says he has made it all known to us, then he says that he hasn't. How are we to reconcile these statements?

What we today assume is that we have been conscious of all Jesus "made known to" us, without realizing that Jesus planted into humanity some things in a conscious way and some in a subconscious, or preferably superconscious, way. When we come to understand this, we will again put back into the Apostle's Creed the scripturally supported phrase excluded in modern thought, "he descended to the dead," for we will then understand that something happened in the deed of Christ that planted in all human souls, whether then living or between lives, the seed of spiritual redemption. As Matthew's parable says (Mt 13,37), the Christ was the sower of that seed, but it had to lie dormant in us until the proper time for it to come forth in knowledge of Truth.[13]

---

13. Christ's "descent to the dead" (sometimes termed to "hell," and sometimes as his having "preached to the dead") found in Christianity's most ancient Creed (the Apostles'), if one reflects upon it, is a strong indicator of the reality of reincarnation. In the latter there is an obvious reason for his descent, but without it there is little (though it has been rationalized). *(continued on following page)*

With this understanding, we can see that Jesus both "revealed" it then and, through the Spirit of Truth, would bring it into our consciousness at the proper future time in human development.[14] The earthly spokesman for this Spirit of Truth in our time was Rudolf Steiner—the true prophet who has indeed been treated like the prophets of old, ignored and persecuted. But he was only the spokesman. The Spirit of Truth can well be considered to be the Archangel Michael—or the Holy Spirit acting through Michael at its right hand.

In our bewitchment with the so-called "scientific" age, and probably starting theologically with Calvin, we have trashed the idea of angels, archangels and all the hierarchies, and lump everything in the spiritual world under the catchall name "God." Some are beginning in our time to speak again of angels, but more in a desire to go back to biblical language than with understanding of their nature and function. Nevertheless, it is a hopeful sign.

What is clear to anyone who delves into the matter is that the hierarchies, and the archangels in particular, are deeply entrenched in ancient Christian theology, starting no later than with Paul and Dionysius the Areopagite. Official Roman Catholic doctrine even today recognizes the three mentioned in scripture, Michael, Gabriel and Raphael (Raphael is in the apocryphal Tobit). Judaism, Christianity and Islam all recognize Michael as the leader of the Archangels and the one associated with the Sun.

13. *(continued from previous page)* The fact that it faded from use is understandable in a Church that has lost the reality itself. Passages relied upon in support of the doctrine of such "descent" and "preaching" include Eph 4,9-10; 1 Pet 3,18-19; 4,6. Consider also Jn 5,28. See generally, *The Anchor Bible Dictionary*, Vol. 2, NY, Doubleday, pp. 145-158, "Descent to the Underworld."

14. In coming to this understanding, we need not strain over the fact that Christ's "descent to the dead" after his Crucifixion had not yet occurred when he spoke the words "I have made known to you" (Jn 15,15). The power of Christ to communicate was not limited to words spoken nor to the conscious mind. Non-verbal communication among the living (telepathy) is well known, and the power of Christ to plant truth in the subconscious mind of others in this way can hardly be doubted. And communication with the dead, for instance, is illustrated by an event in Steiner's life. His wife, Marie, was lamenting how few people were present to hear one of his very important lectures. He comforted her by saying she was taking into account only those physically present at the meeting while he assured her that those in the spiritual world who heard it were numerous.

Archangels are, in effect, spiritual rulers within given segments of time, one after another over seven successive regencies, each of 354 years, as determined by a German abbot in the fifteenth century.[15] Steiner agrees with these periods, saying that the last pre-Christian regency of Michael covered the time of the great Greek philosophers to the time of Alexander, who prepared the way for Paul's evangelism in the Greek-speaking world. The early Christian fathers up through Augustine even referred to these as being Christians before Christ.

The first regency of Michael since the time of Christ started, according to Steiner, in 1879 and will run until approximately A.D. 2233. This is one of several very critical spiritual realities discussed in my writings that show why the time is right for us now to begin to understand John's Gospel and how it is that Evangelist John has "remained" until Christ has "come again." *The Burning Bush* shows that the Second Coming is already underway, having come upon us as "a thief in the night."[16]

The prophet Daniel purports to have spoken during the prior regency of Michael when he, in effect, called him the Spirit of Truth saying, "I will tell you what is inscribed in the book of truth: there is none who contends by my side against these except Michael, your prince" (Dan 10,21). In his Apocalypse, Evangelist John refers to Michael as the one contending against the "deceiver" (Rev 12,9). And the Book of Enoch (1 Enoch), so influential not only among the Evangelists but most other leading figures of early Christendom, speaks extensively of Michael and in such a way that his stature as the spokesman for the highest spiritual Truth is clear.[17]

Surely, when Christ spoke of the Spirit of Truth coming, he was

---

15. Johannes Tritheim, the abbot of Sponheim. My confusion in Chart I-19 in *The Burning Bush* on the length of each archangelic regency is straightened out in the Epilogue to my *The Incredible Births of Jesus* at p. 88.

16. Note that it is our present Cultural Age, the fifth, to which Christ's revelation, "I will come like a thief, and you will not know at what hour I will come upon you," applies (Rev 3,3).

17. See the Epilogue in *The Incredible Births of Jesus*. For its influence among early Christians, and the reason it was not canonized, see *The Anchor Bible Dictionary*, Vol. 2, NY, Doubleday, p. 516.

referring to that time when the Archangel Michael would again be in charge of the evolution of human understanding (the time of the Consciousness Soul) when he could bring the Divine Intelligence down to Earth. This was not possible during Michael's prior regency since the Blood of Christ had not yet been spilled into the Earth so as to become a part of its etheric being.

If we look at what has happened in humanity since 1879 we will see evidence of a dramatic cultural shift in religion, science, and virtually every human discipline. Michael has been working.

But if you will think carefully on what has been said, you will recognize that it is not possible to understand the deeper implications of John's Gospel except on the basis of two very critical premises.

The first is the true structure of every human being. This is summarized in the chart above. The biblical basis of this is extensive, as indicated in *The Burning Bush*.

The second is what the Bible calls "destiny" and in the Orient is called "karma." Inherent in the very concept is the spiritual reality that souls can attain the necessary perfection only through many lives—they must reincarnate. The scriptural support for this is extensively set out in *The Burning Bush*, and it is there shown that the Bible from beginning to end cannot be deeply understood without seeing it in this light. Even the passage in Heb 9,27 that "... it is appointed for men to die once, and after that comes judgment," seemingly so devastating to the idea of reincarnation, is not contrary to it. This becomes clear when the function of the "judgment" it mentions and the distinction between "the judgment of the Father" and "the judgment of the Son" is understood. Without reincarnation, theology has no real clue as to that distinction.[18]

18. The distinction is fully discussed and scripturally documented in *The Burning Bush*, primarily in the three successive essays entitled, "Forgiven Sins," "Karma and Reincarnation" and "Lord of Karma." There is a clear and meaningful distinction between the two types of judgment. The "judgment" in Heb 9,27 applies only the judgment of the Son, which is a saving judgment (see Jn 12,47; 3,17; 9,39 and 5,45). It relates to karma. Out of the Father's great love, the Son was sacrificed for salvation. But for those who ultimately fail perfection, in spite of the counseling and advocacy of the Son's "judgment" after each lifetime, the Father's ultimate judgment is one of fearsome justice. *(continued on following page)*

We mistakenly assume that the idea of karma and reincarnation came only from the Orient, for it existed earlier in the West. We have only to look to Plato, and then to the pre-existence of the soul in Origen's work. However, the West was to delve more deeply into the development of the intellect, overshooting in that direction and forgetting its former knowledge, while the Orient stayed temporarily behind with its fading ancient traditions. Christ walked the Earth between East and West, and the time has arrived when the twain shall again become one.

You will note on the above chart that the human body is really three bodies. The goal of human evolution is that the Soul, the Ego, the "burning bush" that is not consumed, will transform these three bodies, over time, into their three corresponding spiritual states. This is the meaning of the cryptic (and generally ignored) one-verse parable of the three loaves in Mt 13,33 and in Lk 11,5-8. It is also the meaning of the three friends of Job, while Elihu, the youngest, is the Ego. There are over fifty scriptural indications given in *The Burning Bush*, but these three are powerful and cannot be adequately understood on any other basis.

The Mineral Kingdom has only the physical body; the Plant Kingdom has both physical and etheric (also called life) bodies; the Animal Kingdom has all three bodies; but only the Human

---

18. *(continued from previous page)* Those troubled by Paul's statement, "it is appointed for men to die once" (Heb 9,27), and who feel that it precludes reincarnation, need to recognize the difference between what Steiner calls the Individuality and what he calls the Personality. The latter is what we recognize as a "person," and this truly lives only once. The Personality only reflects a portion of the larger Individuality which is the "I Am," or "the burning bush which is not consumed" (Ex 3,3). The Personality's three bodies (as to these, see the discussion following shortly in the text) do not ever return, and thus live only "once." The Individuality is lovingly judged (i.e., "counseled" and "comforted") by Christ as the Lord of Karma and suffers between lives for its failures in the given Personality, but returns again as a completely different "person" over and over until its karmic imperfections have been eliminated. This is portrayed in Luke's account of Christ's answer to the Sadducees (Lk 20,34-38) in which he refers to the perfected who "cannot die any more" (vs 36) but who prior thereto, as the burning bush, are raised again and again (vs 37).

Kingdom has the Ego, the "I Am," or the soul. The physical body is the form for mineral accumulation; the etheric body is what gives life and healing; and the astral body is the seat of our senses, passions, desires, thinking and the like.

When we sleep, our astral body and Ego separate from the physical and etheric (life) bodies. The physical body thus remains alive but unconscious. The difference between sleep and death is simply that in death the etheric body also separates from the physical. Please re-read the last two paragraphs before going on.

The Temple Sleep

These raw facts lead us to what was called, in the ancient mysteries, the "temple sleep." When a candidate for initiation into these mysteries had been prepared through various disciplines, the priest (hierophant) then led the candidate into a cave or tomb where he or she was put to sleep. While human bodies have densified to the point that this is not possible today, it was possible in ancient times for the priest to also cause the etheric body to leave the initiate for three and a half days. During this time it was joined to the astral body and received through it impressions from the spiritual world. When the etheric body was brought back into the physical, the initiate was awakened by the priest and remembered what was experienced in the spiritual world. But while the etheric body was out of the physical, the latter would have appeared to an outsider to be dead.

And just as Buddha was said to have received enlightenment under the bodhi tree, so also in biblical language was it received "under the fig tree." Christ's cursing the fig tree cannot be understood except in the light that this method of initiation was ending. We can begin to comprehend what *the Song* meant by the "beloved" being "awakened under the apple tree" to the love that pleases (Song 8,4-5).

This method is called, eight times in the Bible, a "three days' journey." Jacob, Moses and Jonah all go through this experience.

It is the "sign of Jonah" that applies to both the raising of Lazarus and then of Christ himself.[19]

Lazarus was thought to have been dead, but Christ was serving as the priest, at a time when it was quite dangerous to undertake this type of initiation, and caused the etheric body of Lazarus to re-enter him before he came out of the tomb. This was the raising of Lazarus, and he emerged with spiritual insights that none of the other disciples had.[20, 21]

19. While it applied to both, the resuscitations differed. Jonah's was that of the ancient "temple sleep." Christ's was that of actual death. One of the earliest of Steiner's spiritual writings in the twentieth century was *Christianity as Mystical Fact* (1902). In that book he showed how the Passion, Death and Resurrection of Jesus Christ was an enactment by him of the ancient mysteries upon the stage of the Earth for all to see. The synoptic Gospels relate the "sign of Jonah" to Christ's Death, Burial and Resurrection (Mt 12,38-40; Lk 11,29-30). John's Gospel, in calling the raising of Lazarus a "sign" (Jn 12,18), clearly brings the latter within the "sign of Jonah" reference.

20. This same Lazarus, as John, himself referred to such ancient three-and-a-half-day temple sleep in Rev 11,9-12.

21. There is a quizzical juxtaposition of verses five and six in Jn 11. Verse five says "Now Jesus loved ... Lazarus." And then a non sequitur follows immediately in verse six, "So when he heard that he was ill, he stayed two days longer in the place where he was." This has always jolted the theologians to extrude queer expositions. One of these is so that Lazarus would definitely be dead and the action of Jesus would be enhanced thereby. Another is that Jesus had his own agenda and didn't change it for anything, even the illness of his closest friend. Neither of these sounds either characteristic or worthy of Jesus. Moreover, the first flies in the face of Jesus' archetypal refusal, during his temptations, to exploit his powers to perform miracles to impress others, as well as the fact that he hid so many of his "mighty works" from outsiders. The second is in conflict with his seeming readiness to help wherever and whenever help was needed. What is now crystal clear is that Lazarus had been, or was being, initiated by Christ through the ancient temple sleep that had to run its term. When he says in verse 15, "I am glad I was not there," he is saying that had he been there he could not have raised Lazarus for the additional two days anyhow, and they would have quickly become disenchanted with his impotent presence." As explained in *The Burning Bush*, every "three days' journey" is traditionally three and a half days, and every three-and-a-half-day period occupies part of at least "four days." Similarly, Christ called his own coming Temple period "three days," whereas we know that, while it occupied part of three days, it was really only about a day and a half.

When one was said to have been "loved" by the teacher and initiator, it meant that this one was the one most highly initiated by him. So when John's Gospel speaks of "the disciple whom Jesus loved," it was speaking of Lazarus. This phrase was never used before Jn 11, but commenced to be used immediately thereafter. This is the first and most important thing we have to remember in unveiling Evangelist John—it refers to Lazarus, whose name was changed when he had gone through this experience, just as others in the Bible had their names changed under similar circumstances, not the least of whom were Simon who became Peter, and Saul who became Paul—but there were many others.

To the best of my recollection, every resuscitation in the Bible, Old Testament and New, involves this ancient initiation procedure, with one exception we shall presently discuss. We will now look at how this truth is further disclosed in scripture.

Peter, James and John

We cannot see how powerfully the scriptures point to Lazarus without first going through the threesome, Peter, James and John. Jesus selected these three for special elevation. On three very special occasions, he took them apart from the others. (For present purposes, we may ignore two others mentioned only in Mark's Gospel where Andrew went with them.)

The important thing about these three instances is that they portray an increasing sequence of Jesus' attempt to bring the three disciples to a higher level of spiritual consciousness. The first of these is the raising of Jairus's daughter, the second is the Transfiguration, and the third occurs in the Garden of Gethsemane. Surprisingly, all three are found in all three synoptic Gospels while none is found in John's Gospel—the reason being that while Zebedee John was present for all three, the Evangelist John was not present for any.

Something very special is being told to us by the *sequence* of these three events. We shall see in them a progressive failure on the part of Peter, James and John to reach the level of spiritual insight required for going all the way to the Cross with Jesus in their spiritual consciousness. And we shall see at what point Jesus recognizes this and initiates Lazarus for that purpose. Peter, James and John represented humanity in the Cultural Age of the Lamb, while John was prepared to represent it in the Cultural Age of the Fishes (Pisces), our present age.[22]

Let us look first at the raising of Jairus' daughter. She is said to be

22. This understanding then brings certain other points previously hidden in scripture to our attention. The only disciples specifically called to be "fishers of men" were Peter and his brother Andrew (Mt 4,18-19; Mk 1,16-17), though apparently Peter was the primary focus of this invitation, for Luke addresses only Peter and not Andrew in this call (Lk 5,10). However, the Zebedee brothers were called in such close proximity, and were identified also as fishermen, so including them in the metaphorical class "fishers of men" may be fairly implied. Andrew's presence in Matthew is also fairly attributable to Mark's Gospel which, in turn, reflects Mark's stewardship under Peter. If one simmers all this in contemplation for a while, the picture can evolve of Peter, James and John being called by Jesus for special initiation looking out into the future Age of the Fishes, the Age of Pisces.

That they failed, and thus were confined in their service to the Age of Aries, the Lamb, is indicated by the incredibly deep final chapter of John's Gospel, probably added by the Evangelist himself in Ephesus very late in his life. In Jn 21, the third appearance of Christ to the disciples is portrayed in a scene involving fish, but in a most mystical setting (a later footnote shows that all the Resurrection appearances of Christ in Galilee were out-of-body experiences). They partook of fish with Christ, understanding that it was the Christ, but "none of the disciples dared ask him, 'Who are you?'" (Jn 21,12). It would be in the Cultural Age of Pisces, not Aries, when humanity would be ready to ask the question, "Who are you?"

Immediately thereafter (Jn 21,15-19) in Christ's three questions to Peter (corresponding to Peter's three earlier denials) about his love, Christ thrice tells Peter to feed and tend his lambs and sheep. That this calls upon him to minister to humanity in the Cultural Age of Aries is then indicated by the dialogue in Jn 21,20-23 that points to Lazarus/John as the one who would administer to humanity in the Cultural Age of Pisces, the Fishes.

Finally, as a basis for their understanding that it was the Christ who ate with them, note that immediately before they communed with him, Peter brought them one hundred fifty-three fish (Jn 20,11). The esoteric significance of the otherwise puzzling number must be deciphered by adding the digits. When the one, five and three are added they total nine, the full ninefold nature of the "one like a son of man" reflected by the nine characteristics (three times three; e.g., 1. long robe, golden girdle and snow-white hair; 2. flaming eyes, burnished bronze-like feet and voice like many waters; 3. seven stars, two-edged sword and sun shining in full strength) in Evangelist John's Apocalypse (Rev 1,13-16; see *The Burning Bush*, pp. 16, 151, 187, 214, 433 and 646). This is the basis for their communion and knowledge that "it was the Lord" (Jn 21,12).

twelve years old and the event is reported in all three synoptics right after the account of the woman who had had a continual menstrual discharge for *twelve years.* We have here two women, undoubtedly with a karmic connection, where Jesus was able to transfer the hormonal excess from the one to the other. The young girl was dying[23] because she was unable to develop into womanhood. The power of healing both of them in this manner required high spiritual insights into their karma of such a nature that Jesus told those present to say nothing of it to others. But he wanted Peter, James and John to see it. The second event is the Transfiguration. It was on a "mountain." This term (mountain) almost always means a state of higher spiritual consciousness, and Jesus is often said, as here, to have "led them up" (Mt 17,1; Mk 9,2). You know what they experienced there, seeing Jesus "transformed" and seeing the spirits of Moses and Elijah. We will come back to this Transfiguration experience because it is the key to our understanding.

The third event is in the Garden of Gethsemane where all three of them slept through the event in three installments. They may have actually slept physically. But if so it was only an outward manifestation of something much more significant. The meaning of their sleeping here is that they had lost any consciousness of the spiritual drama that was taking place in the passion of Christ. They had, by this time, totally lost spiritual contact and were only bodily present there.

So now we must return to the Transfiguration.

The first thing we note is that immediately before the Transfiguration Christ asks all his disciples who men say that he is. It is here that Peter recognizes that Jesus embodies the Christ Spirit (Mt 16,16-18; Mk 8,29; Lk 9,20). Because of that Jesus begins to tell them how he must be crucified, whereupon Peter rejects the idea.

23. Lk 8,42, "was dying"; Mk 5,23, "is at the point of death"; Mt 9,18, "has just died"; but in all three Jesus says she is not dead, but sleeping (Lk 8,52; Mk 5,39; Mt 9,24); cf. this with the "temple sleep" above, particularly in Lk 8,54-55 where Christ took her by the hand and called out and her spirit returned (see the "secret gospel" of Mark below). First there was a touching by the woman and then a touching of the girl.

This is the first indication of Peter's failing consciousness—Christ speaks harshly to him (Mt 16,22-23).

Then we come to the Transfiguration itself and we are told that Jesus spoke with Moses and Elijah. Luke tells us that all three, Peter, James and John, slept through this discussion and only woke to see their presence (Lk 9,30-32), meaning, of course, that they were not conscious of a significant part of the main event.

Later we know that Christ perceived Peter's shortcomings and told him that he would deny the Christ three times, as he in fact did. But Christ was aware of Peter's shortcomings long before that.

We must now go to Mark's Gospel because in the light of modern developments it is the most illustrative (though Matthew and Luke contain most all of it too).

Mark demonstrates step by step the progressive inadequacies of these three, particularly of Zebedee John.

First, shortly after the Transfiguration, Zebedee John tells Jesus that they saw a man casting out demons in Jesus' name and forbade him (Mk 9,38-39). Jesus had to explain to him how the action was the wrong thing to do. So by now all three have slept through part of the Transfiguration, and Zebedee John has then demonstrated his misunderstanding.

We move into Chapter 10 and the next thing in sequence is Mark's account of what we know as the "rich, young ruler" incident (Mk 10,17-27). I only point out its place in the story here. We will come back to it.

The next thing in the Gospel of Mark *as it is in the canon* is the request by the Zebedee brothers, James and John, to have a special place on both sides of Jesus when he comes in his glory (Mk 10,35-37). Jesus tells them they don't know what they are asking (vs 38). Imagine the effrontery—impossible in one with a high spiritual consciousness.

Now let us return to the "rich, young ruler."[24] This account is

24. The phrase "rich, young ruler" is a composite description. No Gospel refers to him that way. Only Matthew refers to him as being "young" and only Luke refers to him as being a "ruler," while all three refer to him as being "rich" or "having great possessions."

found at Mk 10,17-27, sandwiched between the deficiencies of all three at the Transfiguration as well as the correction of Zebedee John's improper action, on the one hand, and the bald request for privilege on the other. And what is said about the youth? It says, "And Jesus looking upon him *loved* him" (vs 21). Nowhere in any Gospel is Jesus said to have "loved" an individual save in the case of Lazarus and his sisters, Mary Magdalene and Martha. We have already seen what "loved" means here. It has a relationship to "the apple tree" in *the Song*.[25] It has a relationship to "remembering" whence one came. This is the incident that is reported in all the synoptic Gospels with a significance far beyond that heretofore recognized. It is identifying the one looked up to by all the disciples, and the one to whom Jesus entrusted the care of his Mother.

The Secret Gospel of Mark

An anthroposophist named Karl Koenig, an outstanding, humble servant of humanity, taught a course in Stuttgart, Germany, in 1962 in which he brought this progressive series to our attention and showed how it was preparing for the initiation of Lazarus as the Evangelist John. As one more indication of how the Archangel Michael is working in our Age, it was in 1958 that Morton Smith discovered the letter from Clement of Alexandria, part of which is known as the *Secret Gospel of Mark*. But while promptly tendered to several experts for evaluation, it was not finally made public until 1973. This letter vindicated not only what Steiner had told us half a century before, but also the fine analysis of Koenig based on Steiner's insights eleven years earlier.

25. Three different types of tree are described in *the Song*, namely, apple (2,3 and 8,5), fig (2,13) and palm (7,7-8). Each seems to have a powerful significance. The apple tree reminds us of the story of Adam and Eve in the Garden (Gen 3), the fig tree of Christ's enigmatic "cursing," and the palm tree of the ancient Phoenix myth so vividly demonstrating the cycle of life (see *The Burning Bush*, p. 310, fn 9, and soon to be more fully set out in an essay entitled "Fire" in my next book, *"What Is Man?"*). All are powerfully indicative of the necessity of the human being "remembering" whence it came.

The letter was written to one Theodore who had inquired as to the genuineness of certain passages in a certain edition of the Gospel of Mark. Clement said most were not authentic, but the passage in question was said to be authentic and to belong between verses 34 and 35 of Chapter 10. In accordance with the tradition of the ancient mysteries, however, and in keeping with Christ's "don't throw your pearls to the swine" passage (Mt 7,6), Clement admonished Theodore to deny that authenticity even under oath because not all true things are to be disclosed to all people. You need to know that tradition says Mark went to Alexandria and both founded the church there and wrote his Gospel there which, Clement said, he left in the care of the church there "where it even now is very carefully guarded, being read only to those being initiated into the great mysteries."

Now let's hear what this passage, found after the "rich, young ruler" passage and immediately before Zebedee John's request for privilege, says:

> And they come into Bethany, and a certain woman, whose brother had died, was there. And, coming, she prostrated herself before Jesus and says to him, "Son of David, have mercy on me." But the disciples rebuked her. And Jesus being angered, went off with her into the garden where the tomb was. And straightway a great cry was heard from the tomb. And going near, Jesus rolled away the stone from the door of the tomb. And straightway, going in where the youth was, he stretched forth his hand and raised him, seizing his hand. But the youth, looking upon him, loved him, and began to beseech him that he might be with him.
>
> And going out of the tomb, they came into the house of the youth, for he was rich. And after six days Jesus told him what to do, and in the evening the youth comes to him, wearing a linen cloth over his naked body. And he remained with him that night, for Jesus taught him the mystery of the kingdom of God.
>
> And thence, arising, he returned to the other side of the Jordan.

The writing is widely recognized as an authentic letter from Clement of Alexandria, and the person it describes is widely recognized as being Lazarus.

But by failing to understand what the "raising of Lazarus" was, theologians fail to see the immeasurable significance of this discovery, pointing to the "rich, young ruler" as Lazarus/John, recognized by all the Evangelists.[26] As indicated earlier, this connection was first pointed out, to my knowledge, by Andrew Welburn in his book, *The Beginnings of Christianity.*

Mark's Mysterious Youth in the Linen Cloth

There is general agreement that Mark wrote both the canonical Gospel, the one in the Bible, and this *Secret Gospel* passage. Not all scholars agree which one he wrote first. Raymond E. Brown agrees with Smith's own conclusion that the canonical Gospel was written first and then the passages in question were added for those who were ready for more esoteric instruction, what Clement calls "initiation into the great mysteries."[27] For our purposes, the sequence is not important.

26. Another circumstance showing how powerfully Mark's Gospel is here identifying Lazarus as the "rich, young ruler" is given in *The Burning Bush*, p. 538, in the following passage:

> What is fascinating here is the writing by Clement of Alexandria entitled "Who is the Rich Man That Shall Be Saved?" It is quite verbose, but makes the point that one does not need to abandon all one's property so long as one abandons it as of importance within the soul, which Lazarus apparently did. There is a lengthy concluding anecdote in which the aged Evangelist John seeks to redeem a youth; one can see in it a portrayal of just such a situation as he himself, as Lazarus, must have gone through spiritually in his own youth. *Ante-Nicene Fathers*, Peabody, MA, Hendrickson, 1994, Vol. 1, pp. 594 and 603-4.

Its significance becomes clear when one notes that Mark has Christ tell us how hard it will be for a rich person to enter the kingdom of God as the concluding portion of the "rich, young ruler" account. It is this Clement who, in our century, has revealed to us John's identity as Lazarus.

27. See Brown, *The Death of the Messiah*, Vol. 1, pp. 294-304, at 295 (part of the *Anchor Bible Reference Library*, NY, Doubleday, 1993).

In the *Secret Gospel* passage, we are told that *six days* after his initiation, Lazarus came to Jesus in the evening. In Jn 12,1 we are told that the supper at Lazarus' house was *six days* before the Passover. Since Jesus was tried and put to death immediately after the Passover, these two passages clearly are describing the last six days of Jesus' life. This means that the supper at Lazarus' house followed immediately upon his "raising," as its placement in the Gospel suggests.

Since the *Secret Gospel* refers to Lazarus as a "youth" who came to Jesus "in the evening ... wearing a linen cloth over his naked body," can there be any doubt that the "young man following [Jesus] with nothing but a linen cloth about his body" in Mk 14,51 is anyone else?[28] For those taking the esoteric instruction, these two passages in Chapters 10 and 14 tie together in all essential details—time, person, clothing and nakedness.

Here we must take note of Steiner's identification of the "young man" in Mk 14,51 as the Christ Spirit departing from Jesus of Nazareth. However, I prefer to see this as complementary, rather than contradictory, to the Lazarus/John interpretation above, and in any event not to invalidate the latter. An explanation of my position on this matter is set out in Appendix One.

28. Raymond E. Brown has an elegant and lengthy discussion of the "young man" in Mk 14,51 in his *The Death of the Messiah*. Unfortunately he does not display any anthroposophical insight into the nature of the "raising" of Lazarus as being an initiation in the manner of the ancient temple sleep. It is for this reason, I believe, that he is unable to leave a more traditional view. Invariably one profits from reading the works of this preeminent theologian, and that is true here also. But after looking with his normal thoroughness into the matter, lacking Steiner's deeper insights he stays with a view that leaves the puzzle unresolved.

C. S. Mann, in his *Anchor Bible* volume on the Gospel of Mark, NY, Doubleday, 1986, at pp. 146 and 423-430, takes extensive notice of the *Secret Gospel*, but in his discussion of Mk 14,51-52 makes no reference to it. Being also without an anthroposophical background, it is not surprising that the *New Interpreters' Bible* notes the similarities of Mk 14,51-52 with the *Secret Gospel* passages with skepticism; Nashville, Abingdon, 1995, Vol. 8, p. 710. Williamson, in his volume on Mark in the *Interpretation* series, Louisville, John Knox, 1983, takes the *Secret Gospel* into consideration without indicating its effect on the question.

With this understanding, there is room for much contemplation as to the meaning of the statement by Mark (14,51-52) about the young man, that "they seized him, but he left the linen cloth and ran away naked." It would be helpful here to look at my essay entitled "Naked" in *The Burning Bush*. In biblical metaphor, such as when it refers to "wedding garments," it is referring to the "three bodies" of the human being, which in order to become wedding garments must be purified (Mt 14,2-14; Rev 3,4,5,18; 16,15). One is "Naked" when only the Ego, soul, or "I Am," is considered. One thus stands "naked" in judgment. Since this sentence seems to relate to the more esoteric passage of the *Secret Gospel*, it is probably better to see in it the reality that the soul of Lazarus/John at that moment stood spiritually before Christ and the capturing band.

This is not necessarily inconsistent, as Brown would otherwise imply, with the fact that Mark's Gospel indicates they all fled (including Peter) while John's own Gospel says that Peter and the "other disciple" (Lazarus/John) followed Jesus and his captors to the trial (Jn 18,15), suggesting they both fled Gethsemane. On the contrary, that Lazarus/John did not flee is suggested by the statement in the *Secret Gospel*, "*And he remained with him that night,* for Jesus taught him the mystery of the kingdom of God." "That night" was the night of the trial. Moreover, we shall see that Lazarus/John had a status among the authorities that the other disciples did not have, and thus had no reason to flee them.

We need also to contemplate the possibility that the "young man" dressed in the "white robe" in the tomb on Resurrection morning (Mk 16,5) was Lazarus/John. This possibility has been widely discussed by the scholars, and is not implausible.[29]

29. In support of this we might infer that the "nakedness" of the fleeing "young man" at the end of his six days of special instruction also meant that he did not yet know that Jesus would rise from actual death. In John's Gospel we read that this "other disciple" reached the tomb before Peter, looked in, and saw "the linen cloths lying there," remaining momentarily outside. He then went inside, saw and believed, for none of them yet knew that he must rise from the dead (Jn 20,2-9). While Jn 20,10 says "the disciples [apparently meaning Peter and the 'other disciple'] went back to their homes," it doesn't say they went together. *(continued on following page)*

The Structure of John's Gospel

Let us now look at the sequence of segments that constitute the Gospel of John, as Steiner has pointed them out to us.

First, of course, everyone recognizes what is called the Prologue, the first eighteen (18) verses of Chapter 1. Among other things it talks about a man named John, with obvious reference to John the Baptist.

Verse 19 then says, "And this is the testimony of John ..." According to Steiner, everything in the next ten chapters is the testimony of John the Baptist. Clearly there is no indication anywhere before then that the "testimony" starting in verse 19 has come to an end. How then does Chapter 10 end? Verses 40-42 read (speaking of Jesus):

> ^{40} He went away again across the Jordan to the place where John at first baptized, and there he remained. ^{41} And many came to him; and they said, "John did no sign, but everything that John said about this man was true." ^{42} And many believed in him there.

To see that this is the formal ending of the testimony of John, you need to go back and read the Prologue saying what John was to do, for this passage tracks it and says that he has done it. It is the announcement of the end of what John revealed.

I shall return to this point in a moment, but first let us complete the listing of segments.

Here we have an abrupt change in the story, Chapter 11, the raising of Lazarus, at the architectural middle of the Gospel. Never before have we heard of "the disciple whom Jesus loved," but from this point on, starting in Chapter 13 to the end of the book we hear of it.

---

29. *(continued from previous page)* So the "other disciple" could have remained in the tomb, having by then been fully "taught ... the mystery of the kingdom of God," and sent word to the others that they would see Jesus "in Galilee."

In *The Burning Bush*, pp. 505-506, I show that the appearances in Galilee were out-of-body experiences, in keeping with Christ's charge to them to stay in Jerusalem during the forty days before his Ascension (Acts 1,4).

Probably the original Gospel ended with Chapter 20, but the Evangelist lived in Ephesus until he was past one hundred years of age and he undoubtedly directly or indirectly wrote the final chapter when the need for it became clear.

Scholars have properly noted a very unusual but helpful clue. Not only does the Evangelist not put the name John on his Gospel but, except for a reference to Peter as the "son of John" in 1,42 and 21,15-17, nowhere in the Gospel is the name John used except to refer to John the Baptist, and nowhere in the Gospel is the Mother of Jesus called Mary.

Granted that both the wording and structure suggest that the first ten chapters (after the Prologue) are the testimony of the Baptist, you should immediately ask two questions of how this could be.

The first is, how could Lazarus/John have written the Baptist's testimony two-thirds of a century after the Baptist's death when we have no direct evidence that they were ever together bodily speaking? They could have talked often, of course, though evidence suggests that their cultural territories were very different. The answer lies rather in something Steiner told his attending physician on his death bed. The doctor recorded and notarized it. It reads:

At the awakening of Lazarus, the spiritual Being, John the Baptist, who since his death had been the overshadowing Spirit of the disciples, penetrated from above into Lazarus as far as the Consciousness Soul; the Being of Lazarus himself, from below, intermingled with the spiritual Being of John the Baptist from above. After the awakening of Lazarus, this Being is Lazarus-John, the disciple whom Jesus loved.

The second question is even more profound. If one examines the first ten chapters of John, it is obvious that much if not most of it describes events that occurred after the death of the Baptist. How then could he have revealed these things to Lazarus/John?

The answer comes from Steiner's lectures about the Baptist, saying that from the time of his beheading his soul became a group-soul of the twelve and that it entered particularly into Lazarus/John. I remind you that all the synoptics have not only Herod but other people thinking that Jesus is the spirit of the Baptist returned. I would remind you further that at the announcement to Zechariah of the Baptist's conception, the angel told him that the child would carry the spirit and power of Elijah. And we know that the spirit of Elijah was powerfully afoot in the land after his death at the hands of Jezebel and Ahab. Now if that same spirit that penetrated Lazarus/John as stated above also served as the group-soul of the twelve, then the events experienced by the twelve would certainly have gone with him into the Consciousness Soul of Lazarus/John.

This is a sobering revelation that fits precisely with the Gospel the way it is written.

Let us now briefly consider a few salient points.

Salient Points

Why the name John?

First, it is important that we understand why Lazarus, upon his initiation, had to be called John. The reason goes back to ancient times when human contact with the spiritual world still existed so that the inherent character of an incarnated being was known, and that person had to be called by that name.[30] A person's name could

---

30. The last vestige of this ancient clairvoyant condition pretty well disappeared with the passage of Thomas Aquinas and the other so-called "Schoolmen" of the thirteenth century. These men had contended as "realists" in the classical battle against the Arabists in what is known in philosophical circles as the "Realism vs. Nominalism" debate. The realists contended that for every earthly concept or creature there was or had been in the spiritual world a preexisting prototype of which the earthly phenomenon was a mere reflection. Names were vitally important in these ancient times. Today they mean essentially nothing because we have lost this connection with the spiritual world. That it must be regained, "remembered," is the meaning of *the Song* as well as of Isaiah's plaintive cry, "How long, O Lord?" in his famous sixth chapter (6,11). The reader would also do well to see the essay entitled "I AM" in *The Burning Bush*.

be changed only when there was a true change of character—it is the "New Man" concept of the New Testament, but by then it was only a vestige of earlier times. We all know of these—Abraham, Sarah, Jacob/Israel, Naboth/Elijah,[31] Simon/Peter and Saul/Paul, to name only the most notable ones. That is the secret behind Evangelist John's identity. His name was changed as a result of the initiation, the "raising," of Lazarus—who thereby became John, at least among those with deepest insight. But again, why John?

The answer to this question is also the answer to that consummate enigma that ends John's Gospel, verse 23 of the last chapter,

> The saying spread abroad among the brethren that this disciple was not to die; yet Jesus did not say to him that he was not to die, but, "If it is my will that he remain until I come, what is that to you?"

The "until I come" cannot have referred to Christ's Resurrection because all of the disciples survived till that. By the time this chapter was written, probably all of the disciples had died except Lazarus/John (and possibly even he, though I think not), but that his death was near he certainly knew himself and the last thing he would have done is suggest to his future readers after he was gone that "the saying" was all a mistake since he too had died. So what could the verse mean? Only that in some way he was in fact to survive till the Parousia, the Second Coming.

It is shown in *The Burning Bush* that the "Second Coming" commenced early in the twentieth century,[32] so if this verse is true, then in some manner John had to have stayed alive until our time. The "etheric body" in the above chart is also known as the "life body," and it is also shown in *The Burning Bush* how the etheric (or life) body of high initiates is preserved for humanity in the Earth's etheric realm,[33] the realm in which the Second Coming is now

---

31. That Naboth and Elijah are one and the same, see the essay entitled "Widow's Son" in *The Burning Bush*.
32. See there the essay entitled "Second Coming."
33. See there the essay entitled "Spiritual Economy."

occurring.[34] In this way, in truth, Lazarus/John has survived until Christ has come again. And he has also survived, in a more metaphorical sense, in that his Gospel can only in our age now be read with understanding. It was written for our time, which is also why it had such a hard time getting into the canon in the fourth century. The name "John" came from the Hebrew *Johanan* which combined Yahweh or Yah with "Anna." And the "Anna" meant "grace." The Christ event was an event of grace, as we find in the Prologue of John's Gospel. The name "John" was unique in New Testament times because then it could be connected only with the source of grace, the Christ. In the New Testament, the name "John" had to describe one who was a forerunner or announcer of the Christ. This is why so much emphasis is laid on the fact that the Baptist had to be called "John" in the birth story in Luke's Gospel.

34. That realm should be understood as the same realm into which he "ascended." Acts 1,9-11 reads:

> [9] And when he had said this, as they were looking on, he was lifted up, and a cloud took him out of their sight. [10] And while they were gazing into heaven as he went, behold, two men stood by them in white robes, [11] and said, "Men of Galilee, why do you stand looking into heaven? This Jesus, who was taken up from you into heaven, will come in the same way as you saw him go into heaven."

Steiner tells us that the "two men in white robes" (being the same two at the empty tomb in Lk 24,4) were the etheric and astral bodies of Jesus. The spiritual realm first entered upon departure from the Earth is the etheric, the first realm that Christ passed through upon his Ascension. His "Second Coming" is now occurring in that realm. See the essay entitled "Second Coming" in *The Burning Bush*.

That theologians have not comprehended these things is reflected by the statement (from the *Anchor Bible Dictionary*, Vol. 1, p. 472) quoted in the "Peter, James and John" essay in *The Burning Bush*, at p. 507:

> There is "no incident in the life of Jesus at one and the same time so beset with difficulties and so essential as the Ascension." ... It may well be the most neglected doctrine of the church ... even though it is considered one of the most important themes of the NT, and the heavenly intercession and Parousia are inexplicable apart from it ... and the doctrine of God makes no sense without it....

The practical Kantian outlook of the influential Protestant theologian, Friedrich Schleiermacher (1768-1834), who rejected the doctrine of the Ascension, carried over into the twentieth century and greatly accounts for this spiritual neglect.

Only three persons of significance emerged in the New Testament with the name John.[35] These were the Baptist, Zebedee John and Lazarus/John. The Baptist announced the Christ in his earthly mission. Zebedee John was selected by Christ in the hope he could fulfill the role of announcing his coming again. But only when we see his failure in this respect can we then understand the heretofore puzzling statement of Christ in Mk 10,31, "But many that are first will be last, and the last first." Christ was here saying, in between the "rich, young ruler" incident and the "raising of Lazarus" incident, that Zebedee John would have to step aside from that role and let the last of the appointed disciples take his place, "the disciple whom Jesus loved." This disciple had to be named "John," for by writing his Gospel he would be the announcer of the Christ in his coming again in the Age of Pisces, the Fishes.

The Wealth of Lazarus

The second point is that Lazarus/John was indeed a "rich" person. He can be considered rich in two respects. First, like Paul he was rich in all the ancient esoteric tradition that Christ called "the fig tree." So he would have become spiritually "ill" as this was passing away.[36] But there is substantial evidence that he was also rich in worldly goods. Both of these are indicated by the fact that he was of the high priestly caste of Israel. We note that Luke identifies him

35. Five are identified in *The Anchor Bible Dictionary*, Vol. 3, pp. 886-887, the Baptist, Zebedee John, John Mark, the father of Simon Peter, and a member of the high priestly family (Acts 4,6); but this last (as we shall see) was almost certainly Lazarus/John. The Jonah account (4,6-8) speaks of "a plant" that came "up over Jonah, that it might be a shade over his head," whereby he became "exceedingly glad."

36. In fact one can detect a prophecy of this illness in the Book of Jonah. Christ spoke of the "sign of Jonah" as the only sign he would give to this generation (Mt 12,38-40; Lk 11,29-30). As indicated above, the story of Jonah is the story of an initiation in the manner of the ancient temple sleep, involving as it does the "three days' journey" taken also by Jacob and Moses, not to mention the Buddha. The phrase "under the tree," which I hope to make the subject of a special essay in a future book, is extensively biblical and has reference to spiritual illumination of a clairvoyant nature such as received by Lazarus/John. *(continued on following page)*

this way in Acts 4,6, calling him "John," but not identifying him as Lazarus. Lazarus was one with the rulers. Thus, Luke's Gospel was the only one that referred to the "rich, young ruler" as a "ruler," while all suggested he was wealthy. The fact that Lazarus was one of the ruling clan also identifies the "other disciple" with Peter who "was known to the high priest" and who entered with Jesus into the priestly court while Peter had to remain outside—and who later went outside to bring Peter in, when the maid asked Peter if he was not one of the disciples (which he denied), but the maid never asked that of the one who brought him in, for she recognized him as the priestly Lazarus (see Jn 18,15-18). Furthermore, it was the fact that Jesus had overtly initiated ("raised") this high priestly member and taken him into his clan that triggered the resolve to put an end to Jesus, as clearly stated in John's Gospel (see Jn 11,45-53, but especially Jn 12,9-11) where it indicates that "the chief priests planned to put Lazarus also to death, because on account of him many of the Jews were going away and believing in Jesus." Why was this? Because Lazarus was one of their leaders, a member of the high priestly caste—very influential, and nothing less than a traitor to Caiaphas and the other ruling clan.[37]

Twelve disciples

The third point is that there were always *twelve* disciples acting, never just eleven, even though there are references to Jesus' appearing

---

36. *(continued from previous page)* But the plant was later killed by a "worm" so that it withered, a prophecy if one can see it of Christ's "cursing" of the fig tree. The effect upon Jonah was not unlike that which caused Lazarus to become "ill."

37. This attitude of Caiaphas and the other members of the ruling clan could not, alone, cause Lazarus to be ejected from his position of authority, any more than strong conflicts within a governing body, be it ecclesiastical or secular, can be cause for removal without otherwise appropriate procedures having been taken to that end. Thus, Luke could refer, as indicated, simply to "John" (i.e., Lazarus/John) in Acts 4,6, as being present with the duly assembled ruling group as the other disciples appeared before it. That action against these disciples, however much sought by certain of its members (e.g., Jn 12,9-11), was not yet authorized is indicated by the wise counsel of Gamaliel in the very next chapter in response to the desire of the rest of the counsel "to kill them" (see Acts 5,33-40).

to "the eleven." John's Gospel shows why they refer only to "eleven." In Jn 20,21 it says that Thomas was not with them when Jesus appeared. I cannot go into this as fully here as in *The Burning Bush*, but it was spiritually critical that there always be twelve disciples. So when Judas left the group, the disciple whom Jesus loved filled his place as one of the twelve and could thus refer to himself as "the *disciple* whom Jesus loved." He then stepped aside when Matthias was elected to take Judas' place, for John's mission was to take the Mother of Jesus and to then write his unique Gospel for the future time when it would make the coming of Jesus clear.

Christ's identification of Judas as the betrayer

The fourth point relates to the fact that there were two suppers during Holy Week and immediately before, as John's Gospel tells us. All the Gospels report the second of these, the one in the upper room in Jerusalem. Only John's Gospel tells us of the one six days before the Passover (Jn 12). It was at the house of Lazarus where his sister, Mary Magdalene, anointed Christ's feet with costly ointment. The critical supper, for our present purposes, is the second, in the upper room.

The critical clue to what happened there is in the identification by Jesus of the one who would betray him. Jesus announced at this supper that he would be betrayed by one of them. In the three synoptic Gospels, they all asked who it was, but no answer was given that could identify the betrayer. Note that this took place during the dinner, for the betrayer was eating with Jesus then—as they all were. We also note that even though the betrayer was not then identified, all twelve, including Judas, participated in the Eucharist and the foot-washing by Jesus. Luke tells us that a dispute broke out among them as to who would be greatest, and we may presume that it was here the foot-washing occurred. But please notice that none of the synoptics mention the foot-washing—only John's Gospel.

Now in John's Gospel Judas is specifically identified by Jesus who handed him a morsel, whereupon his departure was witnessed by all of the disciples, leaving no question as to who it was. What had happened to move from the uncertain identity in the synoptics to the clear identification in John's Gospel?

The closeness of Jesus and Lazarus/John caused the latter to be standing outside the door of the upper room with a basin of water, awaiting the certain moment when it would be necessary for Jesus to wash the feet. Thereupon Lazarus/John entered with the basin, and remained thereafter to lie upon the bosom of the Lord ("leaning upon the beloved," as in *the Song*). Note that in John's Gospel this all occurs *after* the Eucharist.

The relationship of John and Judas

The fifth point, consistent with Lazarus filling the shoes of Judas until the election of Matthias, is the relationship between Judas and John. The name Iscariot is related to the zodiacal sign of Scorpio, the scorpion, metaphorically in Paul's letters, "the sting of death" (1 Cor 15,56). But the higher zodiacal counterpart of the scorpion is the Eagle. John was the Eagle, and that has from early days until now been the symbol of the John Gospel. John gives these four Gospel symbols in his Apocalypse at Rev 4,7, and if you will examine the twelve symbols of the zodiac, you will see that these four represent the four corners, lying ninety degrees apart from each other.[38]

But this zodiacal phenomenon pointed to the karmic connection, not only of all three of the John beings, but also to their lower counterpart, Judas. In keeping with that connection, Lazarus/John followed Judas and the capturing band to the Garden of Gethsemane, whence he then followed Jesus through the trials and all the way to the foot of the Cross—the only one of the twelve to do so.

---

38. Since the earth does not have "four corners" or "four winds," these biblical descriptions (for "four corners" see Is 11,12; Jer 49,36; Ezek 7,2; Rev 7,1; 20,8 and for "four winds" see Dan 8,8; 11,4; Zech 2,6; 6,5; Mt 24,31; Mk 13,27; Rev 7,1) should be understood in the light of the twelvefold nature of the zodiac, John's "twelve stars," spread out above us that Abraham "numbered" in the heavens. See *The Burning Bush*, pp. 189 and 472.

The heretofore puzzling omissions in John's Gospel

The sixth and last point is that this all explains why so many important things were not mentioned in John's Gospel, things that until our day have been taken as deficiencies in it compared with the synoptic Gospels. The big three among these things that John didn't mention are the Transfiguration, the Eucharist and Christ's Passion in the Garden of Gethsemane. But we can now see that the reason John didn't mention these things is that he was not present for any of them—and furthermore, by the time John wrote his Gospel they were all set out in the other Gospels. We might even suspect that their omission helped conceal John's identity until the time was right for its disclosure in the Age of the Fishes.

What Happened to the Two Johns?

The intrigue historically surrounding the identity of the Johannine author helps to explain the trail of tradition and legend that has built up around the two John beings who survived the Baptist. And while, in light of what has been said above, we perhaps need not worry about their later destiny, some additional light may be shed and our curiosity to some extent assuaged by looking at it.

Steiner often and unequivocally tells us that Lazarus/John, the beloved disciple, took the mother of Jesus to Ephesus, where they lived until her death. Thereafter, in Ephesus the beloved disciple survived until well past one hundred years of age, until age 106 according to Steiner. On the other hand, Steiner does not tell us, to my knowledge (and apparently also that of Koenig), what happened to Zebedee John.

Much has been made, one way or the other, about the implications of Mk 10,39 in this regard, namely, that both Zebedee brothers, and not just James, were martyred. There Jesus responded to the Zebedee brothers' request for special status in the Kingdom and their assertion that they were "able" to drink the "cup" by saying, "The cup that I drink you will drink; and with the baptism with which I am baptized, you will be baptized."[39] If it could be determined that Zebedee John was martyred, then he was probably not the John, or one of the putative two Johns, who lived in Ephesus. Such a conclusion would seem to greatly reduce the possibility that he was the Evangelist, for the tradition is very strong that the Gospel was written in Ephesus, certainly stronger than that for any other location.

The extensive commentary on Mk 10,39, although equivocal on this point, nevertheless is fully compatible with the martyrdom of both brothers. The early martyrdom (about A.D. 44) of Zebedee James is clear from Acts 12,2. Some have considered that the failure to include in this passage the fact of his brother John's martyrdom suggests that he never died in such manner. But the earliness of Zebedee James' martyrdom and its connection with the contemporaneous arrest of Peter belies that argument. Acts also does not mention the martyrdom of countless other disciples, and especially of James the brother of Jesus, whom tradition clearly has being martyred shortly before the destruction of the temple in A.D. 70. The picture I see is that Zebedee John was martyred as a part of the same persecution. Clearly, such James and Zebedee John were those, along with Peter, referred to by Paul in Gal 2,9 as being at the

---

39. The traditional assumption is that when Christ spoke of the "cup" that he was to drink, he was referring to his death. Only in the lower sense, if at all, can that be so. Steiner has said, and one who contemplates more deeply on the matter must agree, its higher meaning and surely the only one in the Garden of Gethsemane (Mt 26,39; Mk 14,36; Lk 22,42) was quite different. Was it in keeping with the mission of the Christ that he would seek to avoid the Cross? Had he not in fact stated clearly to his disciples that this was essential, and chastened Peter as "Satan" who suggested that it did not have to be so. Was not the last supper premised entirely upon the reality that Crucifixion was ordained as the termination of his earthly ministry? How now can anyone seriously think that he prayed that all this not be so.

When what has already been said in this book is considered, and then when the nature of Christ's body as discussed in Appendix One is taken into account, any idea that avoidance of the Cross was being sought at this late stage by Christ is essentially blasphemous.

Because of the common assumptions tied to this prayer, it is well to quote what Steiner said of it in lecture 9 of the cycle *The Gospel of Saint Mark* (GSMk). In view of its length, it is quoted in Appendix Two.

Council of Jerusalem around A.D. 49-50, though Peter and probably Zebedee John, as we shall see, must surely thereafter have gone to Rome.

Koenig, citing a number of the early church writers, seems to establish that both Johns were banished to an island, possibly both to Patmos (a certainty for Lazarus/John, which adds to the confusion), but that the banishments were at different times. While Lazarus/John was banished under the reign of Domitian (A.D. 81-96), he suggests that Zebedee John was banished under the reign of Nero (A.D. 54-68), possibly in 64. There are reports that a John apparently returned from Patmos to Jerusalem and not to Ephesus, but these probably indicate that Zebedee John returned at Nero's death to Jerusalem and there suffered martyrdom. Koenig reasonably concludes that Zebedee John went with Peter to Rome and was banished from there by Nero to Patmos, returning again to Jerusalem in A.D. 68, after which all traces are lost. But he properly remarks that the similarities in destiny are most striking, and that this fact helps to explain the confusion. It is almost as if providence assisted the beloved disciple in masking his identity for two millennia. But when one understands the significance of the "name" John, as above set out, the similarity of destiny as well as close personal affinity is probably no mere coincidence.

Koenig quotes from Emil Bock (see the recent English translation, Bock, *Caesars and Apostles*, Edinburgh, Floris Books, 1998, p. 301), who in turn purports to quote Eusebius's *Church History*, where Papias said:

> At Ephesus there lived under Trajan [A.D. 98-117] a very ancient man, so old that not only his contemporaries, but also their children and grandchildren had died long ago and the great-grandchildren no longer knew who he was. They simply called him 'John' or 'Presbyter.' They also did not know how to honor him, clothed him in precious chasubles, hung the mysterious emblem of the King and High Priest Melchizedek, a star of gold foil, the Petalon, with the unspeakable name of God on his forehead.

I have been unable to find this passage in the *Church History*. I did find in it that John "was both a witness and a teacher, who reclined upon the bosom of the Lord, and being a priest wore the sacerdotal plate. He also sleeps at Ephesus."[40] (And Eusebius later cites references in the writings of Papias to a "presbyter John" in Ephesus.[41]) The "emblem" or "sacerdotal plate" almost certainly refers to that of the high priest in Ex 28,36 and 39,30, which seems to identify Lazarus/John, for he seems to have been a member of the priestly caste, as indicated earlier. He was "known to the high priest" (Jn 18,15,16), and apparently for this reason was admitted to the "court of the high priest along with Jesus, while Peter stood outside at the door." And he then "went out and spoke to the maid who kept the door, and brought Peter in." The maid quizzed only Peter, but not Lazarus/John (vs 17). And we know that Luke's Gospel referred to the one Jesus was said (in Mark's Gospel) to have "loved" as being a "ruler" (Lk 18,18), implying a position of prominence consistent with that of the priests.

Aside from that plate, the passage quoted from Bock would fit well with Steiner's statement about the Evangelist's old age. But then that statement is widely corroborated by tradition anyhow, and by the very moniker "presbytr" which means "old."

Who Was the Mother of Jesus?

This final section is prompted by two considerations already introduced in this essay. First, the identity of the mother is raised by the third motif from the passage in *the Song* adopted by John, a motif that was an integral part of that verse:

> Who is that coming up from the wilderness, *leaning upon her beloved? Under the apple tree I awakened you. There your mother was in travail with you.*

40. *Nicene and Post-Nicene Fathers, Second Series*, Vol. 1, Peabody, MA, Hendrickson Publ., 1994, Bk 3, Chap. 32, p. 163.
41. *Ibid.*, p. 172.

Second, we've seen that it was Lazarus/John, the beloved disciple, who was at the foot of the Cross with the women, and that it was to him that Jesus committed the care of his mother (Jn 19,25-27). There is credible tradition that the Evangelist did take the earthly mother of Jesus to Ephesus and cared for her till her death. But earthly facts are often symbols for higher spiritual meaning. The late Raymond E. Brown, in perhaps his last publication, *An Introduction to the New Testament*, enumerates six stylistic features of John's Gospel, his third feature being "twofold meanings." Brown says, "In the Fourth Gospel the author frequently intends the reader to see several layers of meaning in the same narrative or in the same metaphor."

If the tradition mentioned is correct, then surely there is duality in this passage, for a higher meaning is widely read out of it. Not only does Brown, in his *Anchor Bible* commentary on this verse speak of a higher meaning, but *The New Interpreters' Bible* (NIB) does also. The NIB, however, notes that the higher meaning derived by Catholic and Protestant interpreters tends to differ. Catholic interpreters have tended to see in this commitment an emphasis upon Mary as "the Mother of the Church, the New Eve, or the New Israel," while Protestants have tended "to put the emphasis on the role of the beloved disciple as a symbol of the church and faithful discipleship."

Without meaning to disparage either of these notions, Steiner gives what I take to be a higher meaning than either of them. Before looking at that, however, it is well to consider what is said elsewhere in the Gospel accounts, particularly in all of the synoptics. Mark's account (Mk 3,31-35) is representative of the others (Mt 12,46-49 and Lk 8,19-21), reading (italics mine):

> 31 And his mother and his brothers came; and standing outside they sent to him and called him. 32 And a crowd was sitting about him; and they said to him, "Your mother and your brothers are outside, asking for you." 33 And he replied, *"Who are my mother and my brothers?"* 34 And looking around on those who sat

about him, he said, *"Here are my mother and my broth-*
ers! [35] *Whoever does the will of God is my brother, and*
sister, and mother."

This passage is a doubly powerful indication of higher meaning
for "the Mother of Jesus." Perhaps according to conventional theological wisdom, it could support either the Catholic or the Protestant interpretation. But only an anthroposophical understanding
of the birth stories in Matthew and Luke can lead us to a meaning
which is higher than either of the conventional views. The complex string of events that constitutes the only account in two thousand years to fully unite in complete conformity the entirety of
both Nativity accounts, is set out in *The Incredible Births of Jesus*
(based upon "The Nativity" essay in *The Burning Bush*). There one
can see that after the Christ Spirit entered Jesus of Nazareth at his
baptism, the Ego (Soul/Mind) of Jesus Christ was not related to
any one human being more than to any other. This realization
makes Jesus' question "Who is my mother?" inexpressibly poi-
gnant, penetrating and profound. The soul that uttered it was no
less than the Christ Spirit, the Dove that descended upon Jesus of
Nazareth at his baptism, a soul with no earthly parent (see Heb
7,3), the creator of all (Jn 1,3).

As pointed out earlier, nowhere in John's Gospel is the Mother of
Jesus called Mary. And only twice is she mentioned, first at the Cana
wedding,[42] then in this passage. Let us now hear what Steiner said
in lecture nine of *The Gospel of St. John* (May, 1908) (footnotes are
mine):

---

42. The transcendental meaning of that passage was fully discussed in *The*
Burning Bush, at pp. 137-142. It was there shown that the seeming awkwardness
of Jesus' remark to his mother is due to the higher message it expresses. The
mother represented blood kinship. Jesus was saying to her, in Cana of Galilee, an
area of mixed blood, that he "was initiating the necessary spiritual change of
humanity's direction away from Blood relationships toward the brotherhood of
all humanity" (p. 142).

The manner of speaking of the "Mother of Jesus" in the Gospel, is usually overlooked. If the ordinary, average Christian were asked: who was the Mother of Jesus? He would reply: "The Mother of Jesus was Mary!" And many indeed will believe that there is something in the Gospel of St. John to the effect that the Mother of Jesus was called Mary. But nowhere in this Gospel is there anything to indicate that the Mother of Jesus was called Mary. Wherever reference is made to her, she is quite intentionally called just the Mother of Jesus. The meaning of this we shall learn later. In the chapter on the Marriage in Cana, we read: "and the Mother of Jesus was there;" and further on, it says: "His Mother saith unto the servants." Nowhere do we find the name "Mary." And when we meet her again in the Gospel of St. John, when we see the Savior upon the Cross, we read:

> There stood by the Cross of Jesus, His Mother, and His Mother's sister Mary, the wife of Cleophas, and Mary Magdalene.

It is clearly and definitely stated who stood by the Cross. The Mother was there, then her sister who was the wife of Cleophas and who was called Mary, and Mary Magdalene. Whoever thinks about it at all, must say to himself: It is extraordinary that the two sisters are both called Mary! That is not customary in our day. It was also not customary at that time. And since the writer of the Gospel calls the sister, Mary, it is clear that the Mother of Jesus was not called Mary. In the Greek text, it says clearly and distinctly: "Below stood the Mother of Jesus, and His Mother's sister Mary who was the wife of Cleophas, and Mary Magdalene."[43] For a proper understanding the question arises: "Who was the Mother of Jesus?" Here we touch

---

43. Scholars concluding that the passage is ambiguous are discussed in *The Burning Bush*, p. 36 where the possibility is recognized of there having been two, three or four women. Steiner's interpretation seems the most likely.

upon one of the most important questions in the Gospel of St. John: "Who was the real father of Jesus, and who was His mother?"

Who was the father? Can this question be asked at all? Not only can it be asked according to the Gospel of St. John, but also according to St. Luke. For it would show an extraordinary absence of thought not to see that at the Annunciation it was proclaimed:

> The Holy Ghost shall come upon thee, and the power of the Highest shall overshadow thee; therefore also, that holy thing which shall be born of thee shall be called the Son of God.

Even in the Gospel of St. Luke it is pointed out that the father of Jesus is the Holy Spirit. This must be taken literally[44] and those theologians who do not recognize it cannot really read the Gospel.

Then in lecture twelve he deals with verse 27:

> The Mother of Jesus—the Virgin Sophia[45] in the esoteric meaning of Christianity—stands at the foot of the Cross, and

44. The literal meaning here is that the mother and father of Jesus, in John's Gospel and in Luke's, are the Holy Spirit and the Virgin Sophia. It is shown in *The Incredible Births of Jesus* that the Mary in Luke's account was inseminated by human sperm, but the event came about in such a way that her earthly virginity, both in consciousness and physical body, was nevertheless preserved and her child was born through the action of spiritual powers. He had earthly parents and heavenly parents–literally. The majesty of the event demands a vast stretching of human understanding made possible only by Steiner's revelations.

45. The Virgin Sophia and the Divine Wisdom are synonymous phrases, and go back to Proverbs 8,22, "The Lord created me [the eternal feminine Wisdom speaking] at the beginning of his work, the first of his acts of old." The union of this Divine Wisdom, or Virgin Sophia, with the masculinity of the Holy Spirit, in oneness, through the divinely guided births of the Jesus children, their joinder into Jesus of Nazareth when the Luke child was twelve, and then the descent of the Christ Spirit at the baptism of Jesus, gave us the incarnated Christ who spoke to John from the Cross. (continued on following page)

from the Cross the Christ says to the Disciple whom He loved: "Henceforth, this is thy Mother" and from this hour the Disciple took her unto himself. This means: "That force which was in My astral body and made it capable of becoming bearer of the Holy Spirit, I now give over to thee; thou shalt write down what this astral body has been able to acquire through its development." "And the Disciple took her unto himself," that means he wrote the Gospel of St. John. And this Gospel of St. John is the Gospel in which the writer has concealed powers which develop the Virgin Sophia. At the Cross, the mission was entrusted to him of receiving that force as his mother and of being the true, genuine interpreter of the Messiah.

This then brings us full circle. We can now close where we opened. From out of the loneliness of the soul (the "wilderness"), leaning upon the higher "I Am," the Christ, Lazarus/John was initiated, "awakened under the apple tree," where the Divine Wisdom, the Virgin Sophia, had been long in travail in delivering the higher "I Am" to him (and to humanity). It was under the apple tree where the trees of knowledge and life were separated, and the long journey of the Prodigal Son began. It was to the Evangelist John that the Virgin Sophia, the Mother of Jesus, was delivered by Christ to show the meaning of Christ's mission of salvation and make the Prodigal's return home possible.

Conclusion

For all who are willing to consider the matter openly, the above account, based upon the prophetic intuitions of the spiritual giant of the twentieth century, Rudolf Steiner, and the immensely perceptive insights of Karl Koenig, can be seen to present a far

---

45. *(continued from previous page)* Christ there handed down to Lazarus/John the Virgin Sophia, the Divine Wisdom, Christ's own mantle, or astral body, much like the mantle of Elijah fell upon Elisha.

more plausible scenario than any other relating to "the disciple whom Jesus loved."

In comparison with the account in *The Burning Bush*, I have had to leave out many things (though several are also added), hitting only high points. Hopefully those are enough to reveal the unspeakable majesty of the mystery of Evangelist John.

Appendix One

*To the section entitled "Mark's Mysterious Youth
in the Linen Cloth"*

In the text, note was taken that Steiner identified the "young man" in Mk 14,51 as the Christ Spirit departing from Jesus of Nazareth. As there indicated, I shall here give the reasons why I suggest that it is complementary and not contradictory to my position that such passage seems clearly to refer to Lazarus/John.

Central to the marriage of both these versions into one is the remarkable disclosure by Steiner (and as far as I am aware, only by him) that no mineral-physical human body could ever house the Christ Spirit for more than three years because of its immense, searing spiritual power, so to speak. The Christ Spirit entered into Jesus of Nazareth at his Baptism in the Jordan when his own Ego withdrew to surrender his highly developed three bodies to Christ (cf. Heb 10,5b, "a body thou hast prepared for me"; Mt 3,16; Mk 1,10; Lk 3,22; Jn 1,32). Earthly death had to occur within three years.

On this as well as on other matters, I am indebted to Michael A. Streicher, of Wilmington, Delaware, whose father, J. S. Streicher, worked closely with Steiner on agricultural matters. Mike called my attention to a lecture by Steiner in Munich on January 9, 1912, a portion of which he had translated for a study group in which he and one of our sons is active. It is identified in the Steiner archives as GA-130, and he calls the lecture, "The Esoteric Christianity of Christian Rosenkreutz." (This is not the same lecture as another of the same date and place listed in the bibliography in *The Burning Bush.*) Shortly after I had delivered the lecture upon which this book is based, he gave me a copy of his translation, which is very close to the one in the extract below. The following passage from the lecture is taken from *Cosmic Ego and Human Ego* (CEHE), NY, Anthroposophic Press, and London, Rudolf Steiner Publishing Co.,

1941, long out of print but available from the Rudolf Steiner Library at Ghent, NY:

> Jesus of Nazareth stood by the Jordan. His ego separated from the physical body, the etheric body and the astral body, and the macrocosmic Christ Being came down, took possession of these three bodies, and then lived until the 3rd of April of the year 33—as we have been able to determine. But it was a different kind of life; for, beginning from the baptism, this life of Christ in the body of Jesus of Nazareth was a slow process of dying. With each advancing period of time during these three years, something of the sheaths of Jesus of Nazareth died away, so to speak. Slowly these sheaths died, so that after three years the entire body of Jesus of Nazareth was already close to the condition of a corpse, and was only held together by the power of the macrocosmic Christ Being. You must not suppose that this body in which the Christ dwelt was like any other body— let us say a year and a half after the John baptism in the Jordan; it was in such a state that an ordinary human soul would have felt at once that it was falling away from him—because it could only be held together by the powerful macrocosmic Christ Being. It was a constant, slow dying, which continued through three years. And this body had reached the verge of dissolution when the Mystery of Golgotha took place. Then it was only necessary that those people mentioned in the narrative should come to the body with their strange preparation of spices and bring about a chemical union between these special substances and the body of Jesus of Nazareth, in which the macrocosmic Christ Being had dwelt for three years, and then that they should place it in the grave. Very little was needed then to cause this body to become dust; and the Christ Spirit clothed Himself with an etheric body condensed, one might say, to physical visibility. So the risen Christ was enveloped in an etheric body condensed to physical visibility; and thus He went about and appeared to those to whom He could appear. He was not visible to everyone, because it was actually only a

condensed etheric body which the Christ bore after the resurrection; but that which had been placed in the grave disintegrated and became dust. And according to the latest occult investigations, it is confirmed that there was an earthquake. It was astonishing to me to discover, after I had found from occult investigation that an earthquake had taken place, that this is indicated in the Matthew Gospel. The earth divided and the dust of the corpse fell in, and became united with the entire substance of the earth. In consequence of the violent shaking of the earth, the cloths were placed as they were said to have been found, according to the description in the John Gospel. It is wonderfully described in the Gospel of St. John.

I experienced a unique joy in reading this passage, for it resolved for me a puzzle that had existed from early in my studies of Steiner. The first anthroposophical meeting of any sort that I attended was a meditation conference at the Ghost Ranch in New Mexico in about 1990. During a question and answer period, I asked the then general secretary of the Anthroposophical Society in America, the late Werner Glas, how Steiner's version of what happened to the mineral-physical body of Jesus as set out in his lecture *From Jesus to Christ* (JTC), rev. ed., London, Rudolf Steiner Press, 1973 (Lect. 8; Oct. 12, 1911) could be reconciled with the version he gave two years later in the cycle *The Fifth Gospel* (FG), 2d ed., London, Rudolf Steiner Press, 1968 (Lect. 2, Oct. 2, 1913). In JTC he had given the "dust" version, and in FG he had given the "earthquake" version, both as set out in the above extract from CEHE. The two seemed incompatible to me early in my studies. Glas could not answer the question other than to say that normally where one sees a seeming contradiction in Steiner's works, one should read on and will thus find them not to be contradictory. I had already experienced that in the short period of months since I began studying Steiner, but until I read the above excerpt I had never found a resolution. I once posed a suggested answer to a prominent anthroposophical author from Europe (Otto Wolff, M.D.) who doubted my suggestion but gave me no further solution. Now, with this extract, coming only three months after the earlier JTC lecture, Steiner has already given the version later to be found in FG and has done so in a manner so as to bring them together. I had already concluded the same thing in my mind, though it was not the same suggestion I made to Wolff, nor was I overly confident that it would be Steiner's answer. One who has not gone through this type of struggle with Steiner's works can hardly understand the scope of my joy at finding his answer so simply set forth.

It is on the basis of just such experiences as this that I have suggested that the two versions of the identity of the "young man" in Mk 14,51 are complementary rather than contradictory.

The "dust" from the above version was more fully explained in JTC. After explaining how such an advanced "body" was prepared for the entry of the Christ into Jesus of Nazareth at thirty years of age (see my *The Incredible Births of Jesus*), Steiner gives the following fuller account of the "dust" version:

> During these three years, from the Baptism by John in Jordan onwards to the Mystery of Golgotha, the development of the physical body, the etheric body and the astral body was quite different from the bodily development of other human beings. Since the Nathan Jesus[46] had received no influence from the Luciferic and Ahrimanic powers, the possibility was given that, from the Baptism in the Jordan onwards—now that there was in Jesus of Nazareth no human Ego, but solely the Christ Individuality—everything which is normally at work in a human organism was not developed.
>
> We said yesterday that the human Phantom [Steiner's term for the unmaterialized human body], the primal form which draws into itself the material elements that fill out the physical body and are laid aside at death, had degenerated in the

46. In my *The Incredible Births of Jesus*, the births of the two Jesus children and then their becoming one in the incident of the twelve year old (Lk 2,41-51) are explained in detail. Matthew's Jesus is called "the Solomon Jesus child," having descended from David's son Solomon (Mt 1,6-7), while Luke's Jesus child is called "the Nathan Jesus child," having descended from David's son Nathan (Lk 3,31).

course of time up to the Mystery of Golgotha. At the beginning of human evolution it was intended that the Phantom should remain untouched by the material elements that man takes for his nutrition from the animal, plant and mineral kingdoms. But it did not remain untouched. For the Luciferic influence brought about a close connection between the Phantom and the forces which man absorbs through his earthly evolution; a connection particularly with the ashy constituents. The result was that the Phantom, while continuing to accompany man during his further evolution, was strongly drawn to these ashy constituents, and instead of adhering to the etheric body, it attached itself to these products of disintegration. But where the Luciferic influences had been kept away, as they were from the Nathan Jesus, no force of attraction arose between the Phantom and the material elements that had been taken into the bodily organism. Throughout the three years from the Baptism up to the Mystery of Golgotha, the Phantom remained untouched by these elements.

In occult terms we can say: The Phantom, according to its intended development through the Saturn, Sun and Moon periods [the three pre-earthly Conditions of Consciousness in human evolution, when the seeds of the three bodies were successively laid; our Saturday, Sunday and Monday come from these roots], should not have been attracted to the ashy constituents but only to the dissolving salt constituents, so that it would have taken the path of volatilization insofar as the salt constituents dissolved. In an occult sense one can say that it would have dissolved and passed over, not into the earth but into the volatile constituents. The remarkable fact is that with the Baptism in Jordan and the entry of the Christ Individuality into the body of the Nathan Jesus, all connection of the Phantom with the ashy constituents was wiped out; only the connection with the salt constituents remained.

This is alluded to in the passage where Christ Jesus wishes to explain to his first-chosen disciples: "Through the way in which you feel yourselves united with the Christ Being, a certain possibility for the future evolution of humanity will come about. It will be possible for the one body risen from the grave—the spiritual body—to pass over into men." That is what Christ wished to say when he used the phrase, "You are the salt of the Earth" [Mt 5,13]. All these words we find in the Gospels, reminding us [that] the terminology and craft language of the later alchemists, the later occultism, have the deepest imaginable significance. And in fact this significance was well known to the mediaeval and later alchemists—not to the charlatans mentioned in the history books—and not one of them spoke of these connections without feeling in his heart a connection with Christ.

Thus it followed that when Christ Jesus was crucified, when his body was nailed to the Cross ... the Phantom was perfectly intact; it existed in a spiritual bodily form, visible only to supersensible sight, and was much more loosely connected with the body's material content of earth-elements than has ever happened with any other human being. In every other human being a connection of the Phantom with these elements has occurred, and it is this that holds them together. In the case of Christ Jesus it was quite different. The ordinary law of inertia sees to it that certain material portions of a human body hold together after death in the form man has given them, until after some time they crumble away, so that hardly anything of them is visible. So it was with the material portions of the body of Christ Jesus. When the body was taken down from the Cross, the parts were still coherent, but they had no connection with the Phantom; the Phantom was completely free of them. When the body became permeated with certain substances, which in this case worked quite differently from the way in which they affect any other body that is embalmed, it came to pass that after the burial the material parts quickly volatilized and passed over into the elements. Hence the disciples who looked into the grave found the linen cloths in which the body had been wrapped, but the Phantom, on which the evolution of the Ego depends, had risen from the grave. It is not surprising that Mary of Magdala, who had known only the earlier Phantom when it was permeated by earthly elements, did not recognize the same form in the Phantom, now freed from terrestrial gravity, when she saw it clairvoyantly. It seemed to her different.

Moreover we must clearly understand that it was only through the power of the companionship of the disciples with the Christ that all the disciples, and all those persons of whom the same is told, could see the Risen One, for he appeared to them in the spiritual body, the body of which Paul says that it increases as a grain of seed and passes over into all people. Paul himself is convinced that it was not a body permeated by the earthly elements which had appeared to the other apostles, but that the same which had appeared to him had also appeared to them [quoting 1 Cor 15,3-8].

More briefly, the later passage in FG read:

> That earthquake followed upon the darkening of the Sun. It shook the grave in which the body of Jesus had been laid and the stone covering it was wrenched away; a fissure was rent in the Earth and the corpse was received into it. Another tremor caused the fissure to close again over the corpse. And when the people came in the morning the grave was empty, for the dead body of Jesus had been received into the Earth.

The passage in CEHE makes it clear that it was the salt "dust" that then represented the "body" that fell into the Earth. The grave would have been empty of any recognizable mineral-physical body even without the earthquake.

The phenomenon that no earthly human body could have held within it the immense Christ Spirit for more than three years is beautifully depicted in the first chapter of Steiner's little book, *The Spiritual Guidance of Man* (SGM), Hudson (then Spring Valley), NY, Anthroposophic Press, Inc., 1950. It is mentioned again more briefly at the end of lecture six (Jan. 16, 1911) in the cycle entitled *Background to the Gospel of St. Mark*, NY, Anthroposophic Press, Inc., and London, Rudolf Steiner Press, 1968.

In the absence of these understandings, theology has been unable to come to a fuller understanding of the beautiful double meaning of Christ's cry from the Cross, "My God, my God, why hast thou forsaken me?" (Ps 22,1; Mk 15,34; Mt 27,46). Scholars are divided over whether Jesus intended to express the words of confidence found later in that Psalm or whether he felt that God had abandoned him (see *The New Interpreter's Bible*, Vol. 8, p. 723). Steiner's explanation shows the reality that there was indeed a victory ("It is finished"; Jn 19,30) and that the Christ Spirit had finally slipped fully away from the dying body of Jesus, for no Cross could kill that, and it "descended to the dead" during the interval before Resurrection morning; Steiner quotes Mk 15,34 at the point in his lecture cycle on Mark's Gospel where he gives his interpretation of Mk 14,51. And he expresses the joyful aspect of it in his discussion of Mt 27,46, explaining that in the ancient mysteries, at the point where the initiate has been raised from the temple sleep, he then exults, "My God, my God, how thou has glorified me!" (see *The Gospel of St. Matthew*, 4th ed., NY, Anthroposophic Press, Inc., and London, Rudolf Steiner Press, 1965, Lect. 12, Sept. 12, 1910). This again is an example of how one passage can have two meanings. Virtually all scripture must be read with this understanding. It was the essence of the ancient mysteries and of all esoteric writings that their "sayings" have one meaning to the initiated and a different one for the uninitiated. The Bible, from beginning to end, is an esoteric book. As an extremely high initiate, Steiner was able to give both meanings. Unfortunately, he did not always give them at the same place or at the same time. But this understanding vindicates the effort to show that the two interpretations of Mk 14,51 are complementary. In fact, both of them are esoteric, and theology has consequently wrestled with them without resolution.

If we now look back at what was said in the text proper about the deeper meaning of the scriptural term "naked," we can see that the soul, the Ego, of Lazarus/John was united with the escaping Christ Spirit as they both stood "naked." It was a joinder of the higher "I Am" of Christ with the lower "I Am" of Lazarus/John (see the "I Am" essay in *The Burning Bush*, as well its essay "Second Coming"). They were joined together in the Earth's etheric world, the world in which the second coming is now underway. This seems to be the clear meaning of the *Secret Gospel* passage where it is said of the youth with the linen cloth over his naked body, "And he remained with him that night, for Jesus taught him the mystery of the kingdom of God." It is Mark's Gospel that has revealed, in its esoteric version, that Lazarus was the "rich, young ruler" who was initiated by Christ when the failures of the others had become clear to Jesus. I am unable to comprehend how he could have used the same language ("the young man ... with nothing but a linen cloth about his body") later with a different meaning—only more complete, for he here ties it more closely to "the mystery of the kingdom of God."

In support of Steiner's revelation about the gradual separation of the Christ Spirit from Jesus of Nazareth during the three years, one other thing should be considered. As I write, I am unable to lay my hands upon a lecture where, as I recall, Steiner points out in connection with this phenomenon that most of the "mighty works" (Acts 2,22) of the early Christian kerygma (preaching) took place in the earlier portions of the three-year ministry. Gradually, as death approached, the ministry moved away from these toward a teaching of the disciples about the meaning of his approaching Passion, Death and Resurrection. At the end he stood as a human body largely consumed by the Divine Spirit, so weak that he could not, as others did, carry his own Cross. That Jesus of Nazareth was the one seen by Second Isaiah in the suffering servant passages, especially Is 42,1-4, was pointed out in *The Burning Bush* (pp. 257, 259 in fn 9 and 511). What also becomes clearer here is how Isaiah also saw and prophesied in Is 53 about the waning strength of Jesus. That he grew up "like a young plant, and like a root out of dry ground" suggests that once he was incarnated he withered under the Christ power as a plant withers in dry ground, for the material bodies cannot withstand the full fire of the Christ Spirit for long. Hence "he had no form or comeliness that we should look at him, and no beauty that we should desire him. He was despised and rejected by men; a man of sorrows, and acquainted with grief; and as one from whom men hid their faces he was despised, and we esteemed him not.... [He was] smitten by God, and afflicted." All this contrasts starkly with his all-around beauty at age thirty (see Lk 2,52 and 3,23).

Finally, in connection with the passage in the text proper where I discuss the "young man ... in a white robe" in the tomb on Easter morning (Mk 16,5), I see this as also probably being Lazarus/John. That Mk 14,51 and 16,5 both describe the same "young man" is recognized as probable by prominent Christian theologians as there indicated. In Steiner's cited discussion of the matter in the Mark lecture cycle, he makes it clear that it is the same Christ Spirit both places. That the "naked" soul of Lazarus/John was dwelling with the Christ Spirit and "phantom" there would seem to follow, whether or not John's Gospel indicates that Lazarus/John went with Peter away from the tomb to his own home.

The conclusion that the "fleeing youth in the linen cloth" is both Lazarus/John and the Christ Spirit, thus making them complementary rather than contradictory in nature, is supported by Welburn's excellent Epilogue ("Return of the Youth in the Linen Cloth") in *The Beginnings of Christianity*. He there concludes, in connection with Jn 21,22, consistently with what has been given herein, that "Surely this is the spiritual truth behind the clumsy rumor that 'this disciple would never die.'" He represented "the cosmic impulse of the Christ." See also Morton Smith's "Two Ascended to Heaven—Jesus the Author of 4Q491," in fn 6 above.

Appendix Two

To the section entitled "What Happened to the Two Johns?"
(From Steiner's THE GOSPEL OF SAINT MARK, Lect.9)

(footnotes are mine)

The first question must be: Are the apostles, the chosen disciples equal to the task of comprehension imposed on them? Did they recognize Christ as a cosmic spirit? Did they recognize that there in their midst was one who was not only what He signified to them as man, but who was enveloped in an aura through which cosmic forces and cosmic laws were transmitted to the earth? Did they understand this?

That Christ Jesus demanded such an understanding from them is clearly indicated in the Gospel. For when the two disciples, the sons of Zebedee, came to Him and asked that one of them might sit on His right hand and the other on His left, He said to them, "You do not know what you ask. Can you drink from the cup that I drink, or be baptized with the baptism with which I am baptized?" (10:38.)

It is clearly indicated here that Christ Jesus required this of them, and at first they solemnly pledge themselves to it. What might then have happened? There were two possibilities. One would have been that the chosen disciples would really have passed in company with Christ through all that is known as the Mystery of Golgotha, and that the bond between Christ and the disciples would have been preserved until the Mystery of Golgotha. That was one of the two things that could have happened. But it is made very clear, especially in the Mark Gospel, that exactly the opposite occurred. When Christ Jesus was taken prisoner, everyone fled, and Peter who had promised solemnly that he would take offense at nothing, denied him three times before the cock crowed twice. That is the picture presented from the point of view of the apostles. But how is it shown that, from the point of view of the Christ, it was not at all like this?

Let us place ourselves with all humility—as we must—within the soul of Christ Jesus, who to the end tries to maintain the woven bond linking Him with the souls of the disciples. Let us place ourselves as far as we may within the soul of Christ Jesus during the events that followed. This soul might well put to itself the world-historical question, "Is it possible for me to cause the souls of at least the most select of the disciples to rise to the height of experiencing with me everything that is to happen until the Mystery of Golgotha?" The soul of Christ itself is faced with this question at the crucial moment when Peter, James and John are led out to the Mount of Olives, and Christ Jesus wants to find out from within Himself whether He will be able to keep those whom He had chosen. On the way He becomes anguished. Yes, my friends, does anyone believe, can anyone believe that Christ became anguished in face of death,[47] of the Mystery of Golgotha, and that He sweated blood because of the approaching event of Golgotha? Anyone who could believe that would show he had little understanding for the Mystery of Golgotha; it may be in accord with theology, but it shows no insight. Why does the Christ become distressed? He does not tremble before the cross. That goes without saying. He is distressed above all in face of this question, "Will those whom I have with me here stand the test of this moment when it will be decided whether they want to accompany me in their souls, whether they want to experience everything with me until the cross?" It had to be decided if their consciousness could remain sufficiently awake so that they could experience everything with Him until the cross. This was the "cup" that was coming near to Him. So He leaves them alone to see if they can stay "awake," that is in a state of consciousness in which they can experience with Him what He is to experience. Then He

---

47. If so, he was a lesser soul than the martyrs who followed him. But one of those called "Christians before Christ" by such as Justin Martyr and Augustine is a special example. I speak of Socrates. Anyone who thinks Christ could have been asking his Father to spare his life needs very much to read Plato's *Phaedo*, the account of the death of Socrates, and then such person will surely be ashamed ever to have had the thought that the Christ could have been a lesser soul.

goes aside and prays, "Father, let this cup pass from me, but let it be done according to your will, not mine." In other words, "Let it not be my experience to stand quite alone as the Son of Man, but may the others be permitted to go with me."

He comes back, and they are asleep; they could not maintain their state of wakeful consciousness. Again He makes the attempt, and again they could not maintain it. So it becomes clear to Him that He is to stand alone, and that they will not participate in the path to the cross. The cup had not passed away from Him. He was destined to accomplish the deed in loneliness that was also of the soul. Certainly the world had the Mystery of Golgotha, but at the time it happened it had as yet no understanding of this event; and the most select and chosen disciples could not stay awake to that point. This therefore is the first kind of understanding; and it comes to expression with the most consummate artistry if we can only understand how to feel the actual occult background that lies concealed behind the words of the Gospels.

Note

Some might wonder why, in Jn 11,35 (the shortest verse in the Bible), Jesus could have wept when he knew he was about to raise Lazarus from the dead. Or they may see it as evidence that Lazarus was dead in the conventional sense, though not so. It is appropriate that this question has been deferred until now. Only in the light of all that has been said to this point can one immediately recognize that these were tears of gratitude ("Father, I thank thee that thou hast heard me," Jn 11,41) that finally there would be one who could follow him all the way to the Cross in spiritual consciousness. Jesus was within six days of the end of his earthly ministry and had not been able to lead any, as yet, to the highest level of spiritual perception (the seventh; see the following paragraph). Lazarus, surrendering worldly attachments, was "able and willing" to undergo the danger of the ancient temple sleep in order to accept his lofty calling and mission. Nor does the later agony of Jesus in the Garden of Gethsemane, brought on by the failure of Peter, James and John to stay awake (go with him in spiritual consciousness) suggest that Jesus was already resigned to that failure. It was one thing to initiate Lazarus according the ancient temple sleep, but it was quite another to be able to initiate Peter, James and John, during Jesus' own earthly ministry, in the manner that would be required of all humanity in the future when the temple sleep would no longer be possible.[48] In Vol. 2, "*What Is Man?*", the sequel to *The Burning Bush*, the essay on "Blood" will show how the Blood of Christ, *Sangre de Christo*, can work that initiation. It is universal, but not nearly so facile as often deemed in evangelistic thought (see Mt 7,14).

As indicated earlier, the designation of Lazarus/John as "the disciple whom Jesus loved" meant that he was the one most highly initiated by Christ. The seven stages of the ancient initiation are listed and discussed in *The Burning Bush* at pp. 345-347 ("Mysteries") and 368 ("Widow's Son"), where it is shown that Nathanael, and probably Philip too, was initiated to the level of having been so "raised," the fifth of seven levels, designated by the name of his people, thus *an Israelite* (Jn 1,47) or *a Persian*, for instance. At least a comparable level of initiation is shown for the *young man* of Nain (Lk 7,11-17; see *The Burning Bush*, pp. 404-405 which also shows Lazarus/John to have been initiated to the highest level, the seventh). These seven ancient stages were also given in May, 1908, by Steiner in lecture five of the cycle *The Gospel of St. John*, and he goes on in lecture eleven to give the seven stages outlined in John's Gospel for the Christian era.

---

48. That the old method of initiation (the "fig tree") was ending is probably also a deeper meaning of the sometimes problematic instruction in Mt 23,9, "Call no man your father on earth ...." Those who had attained the seventh and final stage of initiation, under the old method of initiation, the "temple sleep," were called "fathers" (see "Mysteries" in *The Burning Bush*, pp. 345-347; also 2 K 2,12 and 13,14). Henceforth, all would be called "brothers and sisters" under the Father God (see 8 New Interpreter's Bible 432). The pre-Christian practice seems to have been carried over into the institutional church by the common honorary title "Father" spoken of its priests.

That Lazarus/John's initiation was not yet completed to the seventh stage by his "raising" is suggested by the fact, revealed in the esoteric *Secret Gospel of Mark* quoted earlier, that Lazarus/John remained with Jesus the last six days and was taught the secrets of the Kingdom of God on the last day when he spent the night *naked* with Jesus. John's Gospel, itself highly esoteric, suggests the same by the empty tomb scene where the beloved disciple went in after Peter, and only then "saw and believed; for as yet [he] did not know ... that [Jesus] must rise from the dead." The beloved disciple reaches, at this point, a higher level of perception than he previously had attained. And his Gospel suggests that this preceded the appearance of the Risen Christ to his sister, Mary Magdalene, and then to the disciples (including himself).

Some Scriptures Pertinent to
Our Quest

According to the Revised Standard Version[49]
(italics are mine)

From the Gospel According to Mark:

8   ²⁷ And Jesus went on with his disciples, to the villages of Caesarea Philippi; and on the way he asked his disciples, "Who do men say that I am?" ²⁸ And they told him, "John the Baptist; *and others say, Elijah*; and others one of the prophets." ²⁹ And he asked them, "But who do you say that I am?" Peter answered him, "You are the Christ." ³⁰ And he charged them to tell no one about him.

³¹ And he began to teach them that the Son of man must suffer many things, and be rejected by the elders and the chief priests and the scribes, and be killed, and *after three days rise again.* ³² And he said this plainly. And Peter took him, and began to rebuke him. ³³ But turning and seeing his disciples, he rebuked Peter, and said, "Get behind me Satan! For you are not on the side of God, but of men...."

9   ³⁸ John said to him, "Teacher, we saw a man casting out demons in your name, and we forbade him, because he was not following us." ³⁹ But Jesus said,

---

49. The *Secret Gospel of Mark*, as discussed in the text, is not found in the Revised Standard Version.

"Do not forbid him; for no one who does a mighty work in my name will be able soon after to speak evil of me. ⁴⁰ For he that is not against us is for us...."

10 ¹⁷ And as he was setting out on his journey, a man ran up and knelt before him, and asked him, "Good Teacher, what must I do to inherit eternal life?" ¹⁸ And Jesus said to him, "Why do you call me good? No one is good but God alone. ¹⁹ You know the commandments: 'Do not kill, Do not commit adultery, Do not steal, Do not bear false witness, Do not defraud, Honor your father and mother.'" ²⁰ And he said to him, "Teacher, all these I have observed from my youth." ²¹ *And Jesus looking upon him loved him*, and said to him, "You lack one thing; go, sell what you have, and give to the poor, and you will have treasure in heaven; and come, follow me." ²² At that saying his countenance fell, and he went away sorrowful; for he had great possessions.

²³ And Jesus looked around and said to his disciples, "How hard it will be for those who have riches to enter the kingdom of God!" ²⁴ And the disciples were amazed at his words. But Jesus said to them again, "Children, how hard it is to enter the kingdom of God! ²⁵ It is easier for a camel to go through the eye of a needle than for a rich man to enter the kingdom of God." ²⁶ And they were exceedingly astonished, and said to him, "Then who can be saved?" ²⁷ Jesus looked at them and said, "With men it is impossible, but not with God; for all things are possible with God." ²⁸ *Peter began to say to him, "Lo, we have left everything and followed you."* ²⁹ Jesus said, "Truly, I say to you, there is no one who has left house or brothers or sisters or mother or father or children or lands, for my sake and for the gospel, ³⁰ who will not receive a hundredfold now in this

time, houses and brothers and sisters and mothers and children and lands, with persecutions, and in the age to come eternal life. ³¹ *But many that are first will be last, and the last first."*

³² And they were on the road, going up to Jerusalem, and Jesus was walking ahead of them; and they were amazed, and those who followed were afraid. And taking the twelve again, he began to tell them what was to happen to him, ³³ saying, "Behold, we are going up to Jerusalem; and the Son of man will be delivered to the chief priests and the scribes, and they will condemn him to death, and deliver him to the Gentiles; ³⁴ and they will mock him, and spit upon him, and scourge him, and kill him; and *after three days he will arise."*

Here, according to Clement of Alexander, in what is known as the *Secret Gospel of Mark*, is inserted the following italicized three paragraphs:

And they come into Bethany, and a certain woman, whose brother had died, was there. And, coming, she prostrated herself before Jesus and says to him, "Son of David, have mercy on me." But the disciples rebuked her. And Jesus being angered, went off with her into the garden where the tomb was. And straightway a great cry was heard from the tomb. And going near, Jesus rolled away the stone from the door of the tomb. And straightway, going in where the youth was, he stretched forth his hand and raised him, seizing his hand. But the youth, looking upon him, loved him, and began to beseech him that he might be with him.

And going out of the tomb, they came into the house of the youth, for he was rich. And after six days Jesus told him what to do, and in the evening the youth comes to him, wearing a linen cloth over his naked body. And he remained with him that night, for Jesus taught him the mystery of the kingdom of God.

And thence, arising, he returned to the other side of the Jordan.

[35] And *James and John, the sons of Zebedee*, came forward to him and said to him, "Teacher, we want you to do for us whatever we ask of you." [36]And he said to them, "What do you want me to do for you?" [37] And they said to him, *"Grant us to sit, one at your right hand and one at your left, in your glory."* [38] But Jesus said to them, "You do not know what you are asking. Are you able to drink the cup that I drink, or to be baptized with the baptism with which I am baptized?" [39] And they said to him, "We are able." And Jesus said to them, "The cup that I drink you will drink; and with the baptism with which I am baptized, you will be baptized; [40] but to sit at my right hand or at my left is not mine to grant, but it is for those for whom it has been prepared." [41] *And when the ten heard it, they began to be indignant at James and John.* [42] And Jesus called them to him and said to them, "You know that those who are supposed to rule over the Gentiles lord it over them, and their great men exercise authority over them. [43] But it shall not be so among you; but whoever would be great among you must be your servant, [44] and whoever would be first among you must be slave of all. [45] For the Son of man also came not to be served but to serve, and to give his life as a ransom for many."

14   [48]And Jesus said unto them, "Have you come out as against a robber, with swords and clubs to capture me?

⁴⁹ Day after day I was with you in the temple teaching, and you did not seize me. But let the scriptures be fulfilled." ⁵⁰ And they all forsook him and fled.

⁵¹ And a *young man* followed him, *with nothing but a linen cloth about his body*; and they seized him, ⁵² but he *left the linen cloth* and fled away *naked*.

16 And when the sabbath was past, Mary Magdalene, and Mary the mother of James, and Salome, brought spices, so that they might go and anoint him. ² And very early on the first day of the week they went to the tomb when the sun had risen. ³ And they were saying to one another, "Who will roll away the stone for us from the door of the tomb?" ⁴ And looking up, they saw that the stone was rolled back—it was very large. ⁵ And entering the tomb, they saw a *young man* sitting on the right side, dressed in a *white robe*; and they were amazed. ⁶ And he said to them "Do not be amazed; you seek Jesus of Nazareth, who was crucified. He has risen, he is not here; see the place where they laid him. ⁷ But go, tell his disciples and Peter that he is going before you to Galilee; there you will see him, as he told you." ⁸ And they went out and fled from the tomb; for trembling and astonishment had come upon them; and they said nothing to any one, for they were afraid.

From the Gospel According to Luke:

1 ¹³ But the angel said to him, "Do not be afraid, Zechariah, for your prayer is heard, and your wife Elizabeth will bear you a son, *and you shall call his name John*.... ¹⁶ And he will turn many of the sons of Israel to the Lord their God, ¹⁷ and he will go before him in the spirit and power of Elijah ... to make ready for the Lord a people prepared....

⁵⁷ Now the time came for Elizabeth to be delivered, and she gave birth to a son. ⁵⁸ And her neighbors and kinsfolk heard that the Lord had shown great mercy to her, and they rejoiced with her. ⁵⁹ And on the eighth day they came to circumcise the child; and they would have named him Zechariah after his father, ⁶⁰ but his mother said, *"Not so; he shall be called John."* ⁶¹ And they said to her, "None of your kindred is called by this name." ⁶² And they made signs to his father, inquiring what he would have him called. ⁶³ And he asked for a writing tablet, and wrote, "His name is John." And they all marveled. ⁶⁴ And immediately his mouth was opened and his tongue loosed, and he spoke, blessing God. ⁶⁵ And fear came on all their neighbors. And all these things were talked about through all the hill country of Judea; ⁶⁶ and all who heard them laid them up in their hearts, saying, "What then will this child be?" For the hand of the Lord was with him.

⁶⁷ And his father Zechariah was filled with the Holy Spirit, and prophesied, saying, … ⁷⁶ And you, child, will be called the prophet of the Most High; for you will go before the Lord to prepare his ways, ⁷⁷ to give knowledge of salvation to his people in the forgiveness of their sins, ⁷⁸ through the tender mercy of our God, when the day shall dawn upon us from on high ⁷⁹ to give light to those who sit in darkness and in the shadow of death, to guide our feet into the way of peace."

9   ²⁸ Now about eight days after these sayings he took with him Peter and John and James, and went up on the mountain to pray. ²⁹ And as he was praying, the appearance of his countenance was altered, and his raiment became dazzling white. ³⁰ *And behold two men talked with him, Moses and Elijah,* ³¹ *who appeared*

in glory and spoke of his departure, which he was to accomplish at Jerusalem. ^{32} *Now Peter and those who were with him were heavy with sleep, and when they wakened they saw his glory and the two men who stood with him.*

22 ^{14} And when the hour came, he sat at table, and the apostles with him. ^{15} And he said to them, "I have earnestly desired to eat this passover with you before I suffer; ^{16} for I tell you I shall not eat it until it is fulfilled in the kingdom of God." ^{17} And he took a cup and when he had given thanks he said, "Take this, and divide it among yourselves; ^{18} for I tell you that from now on I shall not drink of the fruit of the vine until the kingdom of God comes." ^{19} And he took bread, and when he had given thanks he broke it and gave it to them, saying, "This is my body which is given for you. Do this in remembrance of me." ^{20} And likewise the cup after supper, saying, "This cup which is poured out for you is the new covenant in my blood. ^{21} But behold the hand of him who betrays me is with me on the table. ^{22} For the Son of man goes as it has been determined; but woe to that man by whom he is betrayed!" ^{23} And they began to question one another, which of them it was that would do this.

^{24} *A dispute also arose among them, which of them was to be regarded as the greatest.* ^{25} And he said to them, "The kings of the Gentiles exercise lordship over them; and those in authority over them are called benefactors. ^{26} But not so with you; rather let the greatest among you become as the youngest, and the leader as one who serves. ^{27} For which is the greater, one who sits at table, or one who serves? Is it not the one who sits at table? But I am among you as one who serves."

From the Gospel According to John:

1   In the beginning was the Word, and the Word was with God, and the Word was God. [2] He was in the beginning with God; [3] all things were made through him, and without him was not anything made that was made. [4] In him was life, and the life was the light of men. [5] The light shines in the darkness, and the darkness has not overcome it.

[6] There was a man sent from God, *whose name was John.* [7] *He came for testimony, to bear witness to the light, that all might believe through him.* [8] He was not the light, but came to bear witness to the light.

[9] The true light that enlightens every man was coming into the world. [10] He was in the world, and the world was made through him, yet the world knew him not. [11] He came to his own home, and his own people received him not. [12] But to all who received him, who believed in his name, he gave power to become children of God; [13] who were born, not of blood nor of the will of the flesh nor of the will of man, but of God.

[14] And the Word became flesh and dwelt among us, full of *grace* and truth; we have beheld his glory, glory as of the only Son from the Father. [15] (John bore witness to him, and cried, "This was he of whom I said, 'He who comes after me ranks before me, for he was before me.'") [16] And from his fullness have we all received, *grace upon grace.* [17] For the law was given through Moses; *grace and truth came through Jesus Christ.* [18] No one has ever seen God; the only Son, who is in the bosom of the Father, he has made him known.

[19] *And this is the testimony of John, …*

10   ⁴⁰ He went away again across the Jordan to the place where John at first baptized, and there he remained. ⁴¹ And many came to him; and they said, "John did no sign, but *everything that John said about this man was true.*" ⁴² *And many believed in him there.*

11   *Now a certain man was ill, Lazarus of Bethany,* the village of Mary and his sister Martha. ² It was Mary who anointed the Lord with ointment and wiped his feet with her hair, whose brother Lazarus was ill. ³ So the sisters sent to him, saying, "Lord, *he whom you love is ill.*" ⁴ But when Jesus heard it he said, "*This illness is not unto death*; it is for the glory of God, so that the Son of God may be glorified by means of it."

   ⁵ Now Jesus *loved* Martha and her sister and *Lazarus.* ⁶ *So when he heard that he was ill, he stayed two days longer in the place where he was.* ⁷ *Then after this he said to the disciples, "Let us go into Judea again."* ⁸ The disciples said to him, "Rabbi, the Jews were but now seeking to stone you, and are you going there again?" ⁹ Jesus answered, "Are there not twelve hours in the day? If any one walks in the day, he does not stumble, because he sees the light of this world. ¹⁰ But if any one walks in the night, he stumbles, because the light is not in him." ¹¹ Thus he spoke, and then he said to them, "*Our friend Lazarus has fallen asleep, but I go to awake him out of sleep.*" ¹² The disciples said to him, "Lord, if he has fallen asleep, he will recover." ¹³ Now Jesus had spoken of his death, but they thought that he meant taking rest in sleep. ¹⁴ Then Jesus told them plainly, "*Lazarus is dead;* ¹⁵ and for your sake I am glad that I was not there, so that you may believe. But let us go to him." ¹⁶ Thomas, called the Twin, said to his fellow disciples, "Let us also go, that we may die with him."

¹⁷ Now when Jesus came, he found that Lazarus had already been *in the tomb four days.* ¹⁸ Bethany was near Jerusalem, about two miles off, ¹⁹ and many of the Jews had come to Martha and Mary to console them concerning their brother. ²⁰ When Martha heard that Jesus was coming, she went and met him, while Mary sat in the house. ²¹ Martha said to Jesus, "Lord, if you had been here, my brother would not have died. ²² And even now I know that whatever you ask from God, God will give you." ²³ Jesus said to her, "Your brother will rise again." ²⁴ Martha said to him, "I know that he will rise again in the resurrection at the last day." ²⁵ Jesus said to her, "I am the resurrection and the life; he who believes in me, though he die, yet shall he live, ²⁶and whoever lives and believes in me shall never die. Do you believe this?" ²⁷ She said to him, "Yes, Lord; I believe that you are the Christ, the Son of God, he who is coming into the world."

²⁸ When she had said this, she went and called her sister Mary, saying quietly, "The Teacher is here and is calling for you." ²⁹ And when she heard it, she rose quickly and went to him. ³⁰ Now Jesus had not yet come to the village, but was still in the place where Martha had met him. ³¹ When the Jews who were with her in the house, consoling her, saw Mary rise quickly and go out, they followed her, supposing that she was going to the tomb to weep there. ³² Then Mary, when she came where Jesus was and saw him, fell at his feet, saying to him, "Lord, if you had been here, my brother would not have died." ³³ When Jesus saw her weeping, and the Jews who came with her also weeping, he was deeply moved in spirit and troubled; ³⁴ and he said, "Where have you laid him?" They said to him, "Lord, come and see." ³⁵ Jesus wept. ³⁶ So the Jews said, *"See how he loved him!"* ³⁷ But some of them said, "Could

not he who opened the eyes of the blind man have kept this man from dying?"

38 Then Jesus, deeply moved again, came to the *tomb; it was a cave*, and a stone lay upon it. 39 Jesus said, "Take away the stone." Martha, the sister of the dead man, said to him, "Lord, by this time there will be an odor, for *he has been dead four days.*" 40 Jesus said to her, "Did I not tell you that if you would believe you would see the glory of God?" 41 So they took away the stone. And Jesus lifted up his eyes and said, "Father, I thank thee that thou hast heard me. 42 I knew that thou hearest me always, but I have said this on account of the people standing by, that they may believe that thou didst send me." 43 When he had said this, *he cried with a loud voice, "Lazarus, come out."* 44 The dead man came out, his hands and feet bound with bandages, and his face wrapped with a cloth. Jesus said to them, "Unbind him, and let him go."

45 Many of the Jews therefore, who had come with Mary and had seen what he did, believed in him; 46 but some of them went to the Pharisees and told them what Jesus had done. 47 So the chief priests and the Pharisees gathered the council, and said, "What are we to do? For this man performs many signs. 48 If we let him go on thus, every one will believe in him, and the Romans will come and destroy both our holy place and our nation." 49 But one of them, Caiaphas, who was high priest that year, said to them, "You know nothing at all; 50 you do not understand that it is expedient for you that one man should die for the people, and that the whole nation should not perish." 51 He did not say this of his own accord, but being high priest that year he prophesied that Jesus should die for the nation, 52 and

not for the nation only, but to gather into one the children of God who are scattered abroad. [53] So from that day on they took counsel how to put him to death....

12   *Six days before the Passover,* Jesus came to Bethany, where Lazarus was, whom Jesus had raised from the dead. [2] There they made him a supper; Martha served, and Lazarus was one of those at table with him. [3] Mary took a pound of costly ointment of pure nard and anointed the feet of Jesus and wiped his feet with her hair; and the house was filled with the fragrance of the ointment. [4] But Judas Iscariot, one of his disciples (he who was to betray him), said, [5] "Why was this ointment not sold for three hundred denarii and given to the poor?" [6] This he said, not that he cared for the poor but because he was a thief, and as he had the money box he used to take what was put into it. [7] Jesus said, "Let her alone, let her keep it for the day of my burial. [8]The poor you always have with you, but you do not always have me."

[9] When the great crowd of the Jews learned that he was there, they came, not only on account of Jesus but also to see Lazarus, whom he had raised from the dead. [10] *So the chief priests planned to put Lazarus also to death,* [11] *because on account of him many of the Jews were going away and believing in Jesus....*

13   Now before the feast of the Passover, when Jesus knew that his hour had come to depart out of this world to the Father, having loved his own who were in the world, he loved them to the end. [2] And during supper, when the devil had already put it into the heart of Judas Iscariot, Simon's son, to betray him, [3] Jesus, knowing that the Father had given all things into his hands, and that he had come from God and was going

to God, [4] rose from supper, laid aside his garments, and girded himself with a towel. [5] Then he poured water into a basin, and began to wash the disciples' feet, and to wipe them with the towel with which he was girded. [6] He came to Simon Peter; and Peter said to him, "Lord, do you wash my feet?" [7] Jesus answered him, "What I am doing you do not know now, but afterward you will understand." [8] Peter said to him, "You shall never wash my feet." Jesus answered him, "If I do not wash you, you have no part in me." [9] Simon Peter said to him, "Lord, not my feet only but also my hands and my head!" [10] Jesus said to him, "He who has bathed does not need to wash, except for his feet, but he is clean all over; and you are clean, but not every one of you." [11] For he knew who was to betray him; that was why he said, "You are not all clean."

[12] When Jesus had thus spoken, he was troubled in spirit, and testified, "Truly, truly, I say to you, one of you will betray me." [22] The disciples looked at one another, uncertain of whom he spoke. [23] One of his disciples *whom Jesus loved, was lying close to the breast of Jesus*; [24] so Simon Peter beckoned to him and said, "Tell us who it is of whom he speaks." [25] *So lying thus, close to the breast of Jesus*, he said to him, "Lord, who is it?" [26] Jesus answered, "It is he to whom I shall give this morsel when I have dipped it." So when he had dipped the morsel, he gave it to Judas, the son of Simon Iscariot. [27] Then after the morsel, Satan entered into him. Jesus said to him, "What you are going to do, do quickly." [28] Now no one at the table knew why he said this to him. [29] Some thought that, because Judas had the money box, Jesus was telling him, "Buy what we need for the feast"; or, that he should give something to the poor. [30] So, after receiving the morsel, he immediately went out; and it was night....

18   ¹⁵ Simon Peter followed Jesus, *and so did another disciple. As this disciple was known to the high priest, he entered the court of the high priest along with Jesus,* ¹⁶ *while Peter stood outside at the door. So the other disciple, who was known to the high priest, went out and spoke to the maid who kept the door, and brought Peter in.* ¹⁷ *The maid who kept the door said to Peter, "Are not you also one of this man's disciples?"* He said, "I am not...."

19   ²⁵ So the soldiers did this. But *standing by the cross of Jesus were his mother, and his mother's sister, Mary the wife of Clopas, and Mary Magdalene.* ²⁶ When Jesus saw his mother, and *The disciple whom he loved standing near,* he said to his mother, "Woman, behold, your son!" ²⁷ Then he said to *the disciple,* "Behold, your mother!" And from that hour *the disciple* took her to his own home....

20   Now on the first day of the week Mary Magdalene came to the tomb early, while it was still dark, and saw that the stone had been taken away from the tomb. ² So she ran, and went to Simon Peter and *the other disciple, the one whom Jesus loved,* and said to them, "They have taken the Lord out of the tomb, and we do not know where they have laid him." ³ Peter then came out with *the other disciple,* and they went toward the tomb. ⁴ They both ran, but *the other disciple* outran Peter and reached the tomb first; ⁵ and stooping to look in, he saw the linen cloths lying there, but he did not go in. ⁶ Then Simon Peter came, following him, and went into the tomb; he saw the linen cloths lying, ⁷ and the napkin, which had been on his head, not lying with the linen clothes but rolled up in a place by itself. ⁸ Then *the other disciple,* who reached the tomb first, also went in, and he saw and believed; ⁹ for as yet they did not

know the scripture, that he must rise from the dead. [10] Then the disciples went back to their homes....

[24] *Now Thomas, one of the twelve, called the Twin, was not with them when Jesus came.* [25] So the other disciples told him, "We have seen the Lord." But he said to them, "Unless I see in his hands the print of the nails, and place my finger in the mark of the nails, and place my hand in his side, I will not believe."

21   [4] Just as day was breaking, Jesus stood on the beach; yet the disciples did not know that it was Jesus. [5] Jesus said to them, "Children, have you *any fish*?" They answered him, "No." [6] He said to them, "Cast the net on the right side of the boat, and you will find some." So they cast it, and now *they were not able to haul it in, for the quantity of fish.* [7] *That disciple whom Jesus loved* said to Peter, "It is the Lord!" When Simon Peter heard that it was the Lord, he put on his clothes, for he was stripped for work, and sprang into the sea. [8] But the other disciples came in the boat, dragging the net *full of fish*, for they were not far from the land, but about a hundred yards off.

[9] When they got out on land, they saw a charcoal fire there, with *fish* lying on it, and bread. [10] Jesus said to them, "Bring some of the *fish* that you have just caught." [11] So Simon Peter went aboard and hauled the net ashore, full of large *fish, a hundred and fifty-three of them*; and although there were so many, the net was not torn. [12] Jesus said to them, "Come and have breakfast." *Now none of the disciples dared ask him, "Who are you?"* They knew it was the Lord. [13] Jesus came and took the bread and gave it to them, and so with the *fish*. [14] This was now the *third time* Jesus was revealed to the disciples after he was raised from the dead.

¹⁵ When they had finished breakfast, Jesus said to Simon Peter, "Simon, son of John, do you love me more than these?" He said to him, "Yes, Lord; you know that I love you." He said to him, *"Feed my lambs."* ¹⁶ A second time he said to him, "Simon, son of John, do you love me?" He said to him, "Yes, Lord; you know that I love you." He said to him, *"Tend my sheep."* ¹⁷ He said to him the third time, "Simon, son of John, do you love me?" Peter was grieved because he said to him the third time, "Do you love me?" And he said to him, "Lord, you know everything; you know that I love you." Jesus said to him, *"Feed my sheep."* ¹⁸ Truly, truly, I say to you, when you were young, you girded yourself and walked where you would; but when you are old, you will stretch out your hands, and another will gird you and carry you where you do not wish to go." ¹⁹ (This he said to show by what death he was to glorify God.) And after this he said to him, "Follow me."

²⁰ Peter turned and saw following them *the disciple whom Jesus loved, who had lain close to his breast* at the supper and had said, "Lord, who is it that is going to betray you?" ²¹ When Peter saw him, he said to Jesus, "Lord, what about this man?" ²² Jesus said to him, "If it is my will that he remain until I come, what is that to you? Follow me!" ²³ The saying spread abroad among the brethren that *this disciple was not to die; yet Jesus did not say to him that he was not to die, but, "If it is my will that he remain until I come, what is that to you?"*

²⁴ *This is the disciple who is bearing witness to these things, and who has written these things; and we know that his testimony is true....*

From The Acts of the Apostles:

4 And as they were speaking to the people, the priests and the captain of the temple and the Sadducees came upon them, ² annoyed because they were teaching the people and proclaiming in Jesus the resurrection from the dead. ³ And they arrested them and put them in custody until the morrow, for it was already evening. ⁴ But many of those who heard the word believed; and the number of the men came to about five thousand.

⁵ On the morrow *their rulers* and elders and scribes were gathered together in Jerusalem, ⁶ with Annas the high priest and Caiaphas *and John* and Alexander, *and all who were of the high-priestly family.*

The Burning Bush

EDWARD REAUGH SMITH

More significant for Christianity in the twentieth-century than the discoveries of the Nag Hammadi and the Dead Sea Scrolls is the growing American awareness of the works of Rudolf Steiner. Practically unavailable until recently, English translations of his works from the German archives are now gradually coming into print.

Until *The Burning Bush* no Bible commentary had incorporated the remarkable spiritual insights of anthroposophy. Now, Edward Reaugh Smith combines his own extensive knowledge of traditional biblical scholarship with years of concentrated study of hundreds of Steiner titles.

Because of its radical newness, *The Burning Bush,* as an introductory volume to a complete series, deviates from the normal commentary mode, presenting a series of essays on terms and phrases of critical importance to a deeper comprehension of the biblical message. It includes an extensive bibliography of Steiner's works as well as numerous charts, diagrams, and cross-references, making this a tremendously valuable research tool.

In an extraordinary feat of scholarship, Edward R. Smith shows how the Anthroposophical writings and lectures of Rudolf Steiner clarify many of the major mysteries of the Bible. Steiner's mission, he declares, was to reintroduce into Western thinking and Christianity the tandem concepts of reincarnation and karma. He substantiates his assertions with his encyclopedic knowledge of both the Bible and the writings of Steiner, which he flawlessly integrates in The Burning Bush.

> —*Donald Melcer, Ph.D.,Professor Emeritus,*
> *Michigan State University, Licensed Psychologist.*

800 pages, paperback, ISBN 0-88010-447-3, Book #2085, $29.95
hardback, ISBN 0-88010-449-X, Book #2096, $34.95

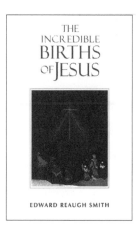

The Incredible Births of Jesus

EDWARD REAUGH SMITH

No Story is so well known, nor perhaps any so little understood, as the birth of Jesus. Its mystery steals into every heart as days shorten into winter. And commercialism's thickening veneer has neither quieted the cry of every soul, nor stilled its urge to penetrate through it all to an understanding of this most magnificent event in all creation.

The Incredible Births of Jesus derives from the larger work, *The Burning Bush.* It focusses on the amazing events of the Nativity, which offer not only hope to all humanity, but a way to understand the significance of the bible as the story of human development from the far distant past into the far distant future.

112 pages, paperback, ISBN 0-88010-448-1
Book #3035, $9.95

For more information on these books and extensive references please visit

www.bibleandanthroposophy.com

For an informative catalog of the work of Rudolf Steiner and other anthroposophical authors please contact

ANTHROPOSOPHIC PRESS
P.O. Box 799, Great Barrington, MA 01230